Making Sugar Cookies

SUGAR-COATING THE GOSPEL

Acknowledgment

First and foremost, I thank God for His love and grace for me. To my Mom and Dad, my Children for their continued love and support and to my love and partner in life Donna.

Thank you to my editor Whitley Covert for her attention to detail which has improved my work, my Friend and author Helen Munday for her example and encouragement.

I would like to express my heartfelt appreciation to all those who graciously shared their personal experiences that inspired the chapters for this book. Your willingness to open your lives and recount your journeys of faith, hope, and transformation has added depth and authenticity to these pages. Each story is a powerful reminder of God's work in our lives and a testament to His faithfulness.

Out of respect for their privacy, the names and identifying details in these testimonies have been changed. Thank you for your honesty, vulnerability, and courage. Your voices have not only enriched this book but will hopefully inspire and encourage readers for years to come.

It is my prayer that, through your testimonies, others will be drawn closer to God and find hope in their own journeys.

With deepest gratitude,

Jeh Howell

Foreword

This book has taken a long time to write. Not because of distractions, but because the message is heavy. I began writing it in pieces, over long stretches of time, with months, and at times, a year passing between each session. This was not from hesitation but reflection. Each time I sat down to write, I did it on purpose. Before each session, I would fast for 12 to 24 hours. It wasn't necessarily a ritual but a way to calm myself, clear my thoughts, and focus on the truth of God's Word.

What you're about to read isn't a theological book or a critique of any church. It's simply my honest heartfelt response to what the gospel seems to have become today. I'm not writing as a scholar but as a fellow believer. I have been active in the church, play in a worship band, and worked in the entertainment industry. I'm not on the outside looking in. I am right there in the middle, sharing my thoughts from inside the church.

This is not an attempt to tear down. It's about waking people up. It's not to criticize, but a call to get back to the basics of worship. My words might challenge some, but they are not meant to offend. I share them with love and humility, aware of my own imperfections and sins. In my opinion, the modern gospel often seems to be just a sweet message that is watered down and weak.

This book is my honest effort to understand this situation and to urge us all to embrace the true gospel in its pure and powerful form.

Making Sugar Cookies

Sugar-Coating the Gospel

Overview

This book uses the metaphor of "sugar cookies" to describe sermons and teachings that prioritize comfort over truth, entertainment over transformation, and emotional appeal over spiritual depth. The book explores the dangers of diluting the gospel message and calls believers back to the authentic, life-changing truths of God's Word.

Table of Contents

Chapter 1: Sugar-Coated Christianity

Key Verse: For the time will come when people will not put up with sound doctrine. Instead, to suit their own desires, they will gather around them a great number of teachers to say what their itching ears want to hear.

(2 Timothy 4:3)

Sugar-coated Christianity is growing in popularity. More and more churches are championing feel-good sermons that skip over deeper Biblical truths. When churches follow this fashionable trend, they risk leading people away from genuine repentance and experiencing the full impact of the gospel.

In contrast, true Christianity is about making real changes in our lives, turning away from sin, and actually following Jesus. This path isn't easy, but it leads to a life filled with purpose, love, and joy. Jesus taught that real freedom comes from sacrifice and holding onto hope during tough times.

We need to get back to the straightforward, life-changing message of Christ.

The term sugar-coated means: making something look nicer or more acceptable than it actually is. When it comes to the gospel, sugar-coating is about focusing on the nice sides of Christianity while skipping over tougher topics like sin, repentance, and the necessity of following Jesus for salvation. It's like when you have a treat that tastes really good but might not be the healthiest choice. Or like your favorite story where the hero always wins and everyone has a happy ending. The sugar-coated gospel can make us think everything should always be easy, but that's not how life works.

While God's love and joy are great, being a follower of Jesus also means dealing with sacrifice and challenges, especially during difficult times. That hero from your favorite story also faces challenges and needs to be brave and kind.

Today, a concerning fad has emerged in which this more comfortable version of Christianity often places entertainment above genuine conviction.

When churches focus too much on entertainment and not enough on solid teaching, they end up with spiritually immature believers. Paul warned Timothy that many would look for teachers who tell them what they want to hear instead of sound teaching. Shallow messages don't prepare people for life's ups and downs and create a mindset where church is just about personal satisfaction instead of growth and service.

Back in the day, churches were all about solid teaching and mutual support. Early Christians met to learn, pray, and remember Christ's sacrifice, not for entertainment. Our churches today should also focus on worship that honors God and sermons rooted in the Bible. True change happens when we renew our minds through God's Word, not just through fleeting emotional highs.

Another problem with this watered-down version of Christianity is that it blurs the lines between what the Bible teaches and what's popular in culture. Some churches try so hard to be relevant that they compromise the gospel.

Nowadays, a lot of churches aim for messages that draw bigger crowds but may compromise on solid beliefs. There's a lot of pressure from society to avoid coming off as judgmental or outdated, which changes how the gospel is presented, often dulling its power. Because of the fear of offending someone or trying to fit in with what's popular, some churches stick to easier messages that sound good but miss the hard truths.

Churches may also try to attract newcomers by only showing the bright side of faith. While this may fill the pews, it often leads to a shallow understanding of faith where people enjoy God's blessings without grasping what it truly means to follow Christ. Instead of discussing holiness and obedience, their sermons focus on self-improvement and acceptance.

While taunted as supportive and understanding, inclusive messages leave many believers unprepared for life's hard moments. A faith focused solely on what God can do for us is fragile and not very deep. When faith rests on feelings rather than solid biblical truth, it can crumble when things get rough or don't go as expected, causing many to doubt their faith.

Encouragement is good, but it shouldn't take the place of strong beliefs and teachings that bring real change.

Jesus showed both grace and truth, calling for change while also offering mercy. Churches need to share the whole message of the gospel without just telling people what they want to hear.

A big part of the rise of a watered-down Christianity is the prosperity gospel which claims that faith guarantees success, wealth, and health. It emphasizes verses about blessings while overlooking the parts that talk about sacrifice and struggle. This message makes faith feel transactional, reducing it to just getting what we want from God. While it might appeal to those wanting security, it misses the true call of Christianity, which asks for self-denial and trust in God through tough times.

The New Testament makes it clear that facing afflictions and suffering is part of the Christian life. The apostle Paul, who faced lots of struggles, wrote: *Indeed, all who desire to live a godly life in Christ Jesus will be persecuted* (2 Timothy 3:12). James even encourages believers to count it all joy when facing trials since suffering helps build perseverance and faith

(James 1:2). These truths clash with the prosperity gospel's promise of an easy life.

People often feel let down by the prosperity gospel when the promised blessings don't come, which can lead to confusion and financial problems. This approach contradicts the core of what the Bible teaches about humility, service, and perseverance. True faith is about having a relationship with God, not seeking material gain. It prepares people for challenges through Scripture.

At the heart of this softer approach is a failure to explain what it really means to follow Christ. Jesus said that anyone who wants to be His disciple must deny themselves and take up their cross (Matthew 16:24). This often means facing sacrifice and rejecting worldly values. If believers don't understand this call, they risk having a weak faith that can't handle tough times.

Real discipleship shifts our focus from ourselves to God. It's about living for something greater and letting go of whatever gets in the way of our relationship with Christ. Paul showed this attitude when he said that knowing Christ was worth more than everything else. A life of surrender to God shows how powerful His grace is and strengthens the church as a whole.

Not having strong teaching makes believers easy targets for false ideas that mix reality with worldly thoughts. Paul warned about being tossed around by misleading teachings. Without grounding in Scripture, it's easy to fall for these messages. The church should emphasize solid doctrine and encourage folks to study the Bible, testing teachings against God's Word.

Another risk with this softer Christianity is the false sense of security it can give. When churches shy away from talking about sin and the need for change, people might think they're saved without really transforming. Paul urged believers to check their faith, stressing that true salvation leads to a changed life marked by repentance and following God. A watered-down message can make people complacent and unprepared for what discipleship truly requires.

Jesus offered a welcoming message but also asked for total commitment. He made it clear that carrying a cross and fully following Him is essential. The true gospel confronts us with our sin, calls for change, and demands a devoted life to Christ.

It's not about comfort. It's about real transformation that leads to lasting peace and purpose.

The church needs to reject compromise and commit to sharing the whole gospel. Leaders should speak the truth, even when it's hard to say. Believers should also strive to grow in their faith, digging into Scripture and living it out. True worship should honor God rather than just personal likes, and solid teachings help believers stand firm in their faith.

Going back to sound doctrine is crucial for the church to fulfill its mission. Jesus' message of repentance and sacrifice is still powerful today. By embracing the full gospel, the church can guide people toward genuine faith and change lives for God's glory.

Questions

1. How do I respond to the sugar-coated gospel?

2. Am I supporting a watered-down gospel at my church?

3. Do I seek God's truth from the Word, or do I gravitate toward teachings that only focus on the parts I like?

4. What does the gospel really mean to me?

5. Am I ready to hear the difficult truths in the Bible?

6. How can I encourage my church to preach the whole truth and not just a candy-coated message?

Noah

Noah was slouched in the back of the church, arms crossed and eyes wandering over the shiny wood of the pews in front of him. It was Sunday morning again, and just like clockwork, the congregation gathered, hopeful for some insight from above. You could practically feel the anticipation hanging in the air as the pastor made his way to the pulpit. A wave of murmurs and nods rippled through the crowd. They were all set for a sermon, but what they got was a motivational speech.

"God loves you. He really, really loves you!" Pastor Evan kicked things off. His voice was warm and inviting like a cozy blanket on a chilly night. "No matter what you've done, no matter how far you've wandered off, His love doesn't waver. You're perfect just as you are in His eyes."

Noah leaned back, his brows knitting together. The words felt overly smooth like syrup drizzled on a plain pancake. He fidgeted in his seat, trying to pay attention, but the speech just kept flowing, each line more comforting than the last. "You're

12

amazing," Pastor Evan added. "Don't let anyone tell you otherwise. God has a plan just for you, and all you have to do is believe. Trust that everything you desire is already headed your way."

Noah looked around him. The people were utterly absorbed, nodding along, their eyes glistening with hope. Some whispered "Amen" softly to themselves. They seemed to be soaking it all up, and for a fleeting moment, Noah wondered if perhaps he was missing something.

But then, doubts started creeping in. Was this really a sermon? Or just a feel-good pep talk? Noah couldn't recall the last time he heard a message about responsibility, sacrifice, or those tough choices that real faith often requires. Where was the challenge? Where were the tough conversations that usually come with personal growth? Everything the pastor said felt so easy. The kind of message that could boost anyone's self-esteem without pushing for meaningful change.

He shuffled in his seat again. It wasn't that he didn't want to feel uplifted, but deep down, Noah understood that faith wasn't just about cozy words that made you feel good for an hour. It was about transformation, the kind that burned away egos, forcing you to face the uncomfortable parts of yourself.

When the service was over, Noah couldn't shake the feeling that he'd been sold something. Sure, the promises of God's love were genuine, but the way they were presented felt just a bit too neat, too safe. Everyone filed out of the church with smiles, looking content as if the pastor had offered them a glimpse of paradise.

Noah lingered at the back, watching people leave with a strange mix of thoughts. For a moment, he questioned if he was just being too negative. After all, wasn't a bit of encouragement necessary? People face struggles. Maybe they really needed to hear words that made them feel seen, heard, and loved.

Yet, in the pit of his stomach, he couldn't shake the nagging thought: If all you ever hear is that everything's fine, when do you get the chance to truly change?

Sugar-Coated Gospel Cookies

Ingredients:

- **2 cups Pre-Selected Verses** (only the comforting ones, just skip anything about sin, repentance, or judgment)
  Examples: Jeremiah 29:11, Philippians 4:13, and John 3:16 (without verse 17 or 18)
- **1 cup Flattery Flour**
  This fine white powder makes everything sound sweet and smooths over any rough convictions.
- **3/4 cup Filtered Sermons**
  Use only sermons free from offensive topics like hell, holiness, or sacrifice. Be sure they're inspirational and easy to digest.
- **1/2 cup Emotional Frosting**
  A whipped blend of mood lighting, powerful music, and personal stories that stir the heart but not the soul.
- **1 tsp Avoidance of Accountability Extract**
  Adds just the right flavor of "no one can judge me."
- **1 stick of "God Wants You Happy" Margarine**
  Melted over self-centered theology. Replace "deny yourself" with "treat yourself."
- **Dash of Half-Truth Sprinkles**
  Optional, but often used to add color and misdirection. Just enough Scripture to sound biblical.
- **Zero pinches of Salt**
  Leave out the salt of truth—it's too sharp and ruins the "sweet" vibe.

Instructions:

1. **Preheat the atmosphere** by lowering conviction and increasing entertainment to a warm, cozy emotional temperature.
2. **In a large mixing bowl,** combine pre-selected verses and filtered sermons. Stir gently, being careful not to disturb anyone's comfort zone.

3. **Add in the flattery flour** slowly, avoiding any lumps of truth. Truth makes the batter too thick and hard to swallow.
4. **Blend in the "God wants you happy" margarine** until the mixture is smooth and free from self-denial or suffering.
5. **Fold in emotional frosting** and mix until it overpowers anything theological. The batter should now smell like personal destiny and feel-good vibes.
6. **Sprinkle lightly with avoidance extract and half-truths.** These won't provide any spiritual growth, but they do make the surface sparkle.
7. **Shape into heartwarming messages** and lay them out on a non-stick platform. Bake under the light of applause until golden and easily palatable.
8. **Cool until conviction disappears.** Serve with a side of self-help and affirmations.

WARNING LABEL:

- **Nutrition Facts:** Lacks spiritual protein, living water, and Bread of Life. High in spiritual sugar, guaranteed to spike emotionalism and crash into complacency.
- **Contains artificial grace and imitation holiness.**
- **Not suitable for those seeking true discipleship or eternal transformation.**
- **Serves: Masses, but satisfies few. Lasting nourishment: None.**

CHAPTER

2

Chapter 2: The Sugar-Coated Gospel or the True Gospel of Christ?

Key Verse: Whoever does not take up their cross and follow me is not worthy of me.

(Matthew 10:38)

The sugar-coated gospel clashes with the true message of Christ. Christians need to consider what it truly means to follow Him. When you look at Jesus' life and teachings, it's evident His message is about surrender, transformation, and the willingness to follow Him regardless of the cost.

The rise of the sugar-coated gospel, or gospel of comfort, is a reflection of our cultural obsession with convenience and instant gratification which prioritizes personal success and avoids hardship. This mindset has seeped into the church, reshaping how the gospel is preached. Sermons are often designed to make people feel good, highlighting the benefits of faith while ignoring the realities of suffering, sacrifice, and persecution inherent in the Christian life.

At the heart of this sugar-coated gospel is the prosperity message which falsely teaches that God's ultimate desire is for believers to be wealthy, successful, and comfortable. Adherents are often told that strong faith and generous giving will lead to material abundance and a carefree life. This diluted version of God's Word seeks to appeal to our desire for an easy life while neglecting the fundamental truth. Discipleship requires taking up a cross, dying to self, and embracing the cost of following Christ. While the prosperity message is attractive, it directly contradicts Jesus' teaching. He warned His followers that they would face persecution and hardship for His sake. The gospel of comfort ignores the reality that following Christ often means enduring trials, not avoiding them.

This therapeutic version of Christianity also promotes emotional fulfillment as a primary goal. While Scripture acknowledges God's care for our emotional well-being, the focus of the gospel is not self-fulfillment but self-sacrifice. True faith calls us to surrender our desires and align our lives with God's will, not to use faith as a means to achieve personal satisfaction. Churches that cater to these desires risk neglecting the essential message of repentance, holiness, and transformation.

Christianity at its core calls for a radical, personal transformation by surrendering oneself to obedience to God and a commitment to follow Christ no matter the cost. The true gospel is not one of comfort but one of giving all, calling believers to live in the world without being of it. Following Jesus often involves discomfort, affliction, and even rejection.

A superficial faith that is rooted in feelings rather than truth cannot withstand trials or persecution. Jesus warned about this in the parable of the sower: *The one who received the seed that fell on rocky places is the man who hears the word and at once receives it with joy. But since he has no root, he lasts only a short time. When trouble or persecution comes because of the word, he quickly falls away* (Matthew 13:20-21). This shallow faith thrives in times of peace but withers in adversity because it was never grounded in the truth of the gospel. True faith isn't about avoiding hardship but trusting in God during those rough times.

Faith grows through trials. Paul reminds us in Romans 5:3-4: *We also glory in our sufferings, because we know that suffering produces perseverance; perseverance, character; and character, hope.* The real gospel calls us to embrace challenges as opportunities for spiritual growth, becoming more like Christ in the process.

God's Word calls us to take up our cross and follow Jesus, not for personal gain but for the glory of God. Jesus said: *whoever does not take up their cross and follow me is not worthy of me* (Matthew 10:38). The cross symbolizes sacrifice, suffering, and death to self. Following Christ requires a willingness to give up our own desires, plans, and comfort in pursuit of His kingdom.

Jesus never promised an easy path. His call to discipleship was one of radical obedience, often marked by persecution, shunning, and even death. The apostles understood this. They left behind family, careers, and security to follow Him. Their lives were characterized by obedience, even in the face of imprisonment and martyrdom. Paul echoed this commitment in Philippians 3:8: *I consider everything a loss because of the surpassing worth of knowing Christ Jesus my Lord, for whose sake I have lost all things.* He understood that knowing Christ was worth any price.

The cost of discipleship is not limited to suffering. It also demands a willingness to let go of anything that hinders our relationship with Christ. Jesus made this clear in Luke 14:27: *And whoever does not carry their cross and follow me cannot be my disciple.* Discipleship is a wholehearted commitment to Christ, requiring us to count the cost and prioritize Him above all else. This radical commitment is illustrated in the parable of the hidden treasure. Jesus said: *The kingdom of heaven is like treasure hidden in a field. When a man found it, he hid it again, and then in his joy went and sold all he had and bought that field* (Matthew 13:44). The man recognized the incomparable value of the kingdom and was willing to give up everything to gain it. A joyful willingness to sacrifice all for the sake of Christ is the heart of discipleship.

While the cost of discipleship is high, the rewards are eternal. Jesus promised that those who follow Him will receive blessings far greater than anything they give up. *And everyone who has left houses or brothers or sisters or father or mother or wife or children or fields for my sake will receive a hundred times as much and will inherit eternal life* (Matthew 19:29). Paul, reflecting on all he had endured, looked forward to the ultimate reward. *I have fought the good fight, I have finished the race, I have kept the faith. Now there is in store for me the crown of righteousness, which the Lord, the righteous Judge, will award to me on that day* (2 Timothy 4:7-8). The joys of eternal life and fellowship with Christ far outweigh any earthly sacrifice.

The true gospel is not a promise of comfort but a call to radical obedience, relinquishing self, and transformation. In Luke 9:62, Jesus says: *No one who puts a hand to the plow and looks back is fit for service in the kingdom of God.* This is a call to wholehearted devotion with no turning back. Jesus invites us to follow Him, not for personal gain but to know Him and share in His eternal glory. Discipleship may come at a cost, but it is a joyful surrender to the One who is infinitely worthy. Whatever we lose in this life is nothing compared to the surpassing worth of knowing Christ and the eternal rewards He has prepared for those who love Him.

Questions

1. What parts of my life do I need to change? Are there sins I've been ignoring as I follow Christ?

2. Am I seeking solid Biblical teachings?

3. Have I actually done what Jesus asked?

4. Am I ready to stick with Christ even when it's hard, or do I just want an easy, comfortable kind of faith?

Laura

My friend Laura always had faith in Jesus. Growing up in church, she heard messages about blessings and how God wanted the best for everyone. "God will make everything work out for you!" the pastors would say, and she loved the thought of a God who was there to help her.

As she hit her twenties, she kept that mindset. Laura prayed for the job she wanted, looked for love, and expected smooth sailing. But then life took a turn. Her job didn't pan out, her relationship ended, and she felt lonely and uncertain.

"What happened to those promises?" she thought. "Where's the God who's supposed to give me what I want?"

One Sunday, feeling low, she decided to try a new church. The pastor started off talking about God's love and blessings. But soon, his tone changed. He began to talk about what it really meant to follow Jesus.

"Being a follower of Jesus isn't just about getting what you want," he said. "It requires sacrifice. It means letting go of your comfort and plans, even when it's tough."

Laura's heart raced. "Take up my cross?" She had never thought of it like that before. She always viewed Jesus as someone who made life easy, not someone who faced struggle.

The pastor continued, "Jesus didn't promise us a pain-free life. He promised to be with us through everything, even when it gets hard. He's called us to be His followers, sharing in both the good times and the tough ones."

As he spoke, she felt something shift inside her. She realized she'd been living for the sugar-coated gospel of comfort, wanting only the easy promises. She then understood that the real gospel was about following Jesus through challenges and trusting Him no matter what.

Afterward, Laura stayed to chat with the pastor. She asked how she could move beyond her desire for only blessings. He replied kindly, "First off, know that Jesus didn't ask us to follow Him for comfort. He called us because He offers a real life rooted in hope. Sometimes that means hardships, but those moments can actually bring us closer to God."

Leaving the church, Laura felt heavy but also clear-headed. She knew following Jesus wasn't just about getting what she wanted. It was about building a deeper relationship and letting go of her desires, embracing struggles, and trusting Him during tough times. Jesus might not make her life easier, but He promised to be alongside her, strengthen her, and help her grow.

As the weeks went by, Laura changed her outlook. Instead of praying for a perfect job or relationship, she started asking God for courage to face whatever came her way. Slowly, she found peace, not because everything was ideal, but because she felt God with her, guiding her, and helping her grow.

Laura's journey shows us that following Jesus isn't just about seeking sweet blessings. It's about fully trusting Him, knowing that even in bitter times, He's at work. The true call of the gospel asks us to take up our cross, embrace the cost of following, and stay close to Christ through every twist and turn. It's in these challenging moments that we find real growth and experience His love and grace.

Cotton Candy Christianity

Ingredients:

- 1 bag of Whipped Emotions
- 2 scoops of Cherry-Picked Promises
- 1 teaspoon of "Don't Judge" Syrup
- A cloud of Stage Lights and Smoke Machines
- 1 cup of Positive Vibes
- A handful of "Follow Your Heart" flakes
- NO repentance, NO holiness, NO sacrifice

Instructions:

1. Spin the Word of God at high speed until its structure breaks down.
2. Fluff it up with affirming phrases and vague spirituality.
3. Avoid any heat (conviction) so it doesn't melt away.
4. Serve on a stick during 20-minute sermons and worship sets.
5. Watch as it dissolves in the mouth but leaves a hollow heart.

WARNING LABEL:

- **Nutrition Facts:** Stadium crowds
- **Spiritual Nutrition:** Zero
- **Shelf Life:** Until suffering hits
- **Side Effects:** A craving for more attention, more comfort, and more entertainment. No hunger for righteousness.

Chapter 3: Entertainment vs. Edification

Key Verse: Do not conform to the pattern of this world, but be transformed by the renewing of your mind.

(Romans 12:2)

One of the most evident trends in sugar-coated Christianity is the shift toward entertainment in worship. This recent fad reveals a troubling change in the modern practice of faith. When worship becomes more of a show, it risks reducing sacred moments to spectacles, fostering a consumer mindset rather than cultivating genuine spiritual growth.

Modern worship experiences, especially at megachurches, often feel like concerts or flashy productions. These performances are complete with elaborate professional lighting, polished music, and multimedia displays on video screens designed to captivate audiences but often failing to encourage real spiritual growth. While these elements do engage people, they shift the spotlight from God's glory to emotional highs, reducing worship to a performance rather than a sacred time of reflection and growth. Worship is meant to exalt God and edify believers, only many churches seem to strive to create an emotionally tense atmosphere instead of developing a deeper relationship with God. Sermons frequently follow that resemble motivational talks, emphasizing personal success and temporary happiness over the transformative power of the gospel.

This entertainment-driven approach risks creating a generation of believers who prioritize experiences over spiritual depth. Worship services increasingly blur the line between concerts and sacred gatherings with more attention placed on the performance of worship bands rather than on the congregation's participation in praising God.

Emotional highs from stirring music and visuals may inspire temporarily but rarely lead to long-term transformation. Consequently, worshipers may seek out feelings rather than the deep, challenging truths of Scripture.

This client-centric mode of operation has seeped into how people view church. Many now look to worship as a service designed to meet their emotional needs or provide motivation. Or they come to worship seeking to be served rather than to serve. Churches, especially larger ones, often shape their services to please their audiences, prioritizing what is popular over what is biblically true. Marketing strategies and surveys have replaced spiritual discernment, leading to worship services that cater to desires rather than challenge hearts. This trend risks turning worship into a product designed to please man rather than a sacred offering to God. If one church fails to deliver, they simply move on to another. This attitude undermines the true purpose of worship: to honor God, pursue spiritual growth, and prepare believers to serve others. Early Christians came to pray together, ground themselves, and worship Christ's sacrifice, not to be entertained.

When the line between worship and showmanship fades, true worship is at risk. While emotionally powerful songs or uplifting sermons can impact people, without a foundation in Scripture, they fail to foster lasting spiritual growth. Worship was never meant to be about how it makes us feel. It is about offering ourselves as living sacrifices to God as Paul urges in Romans 12:1. True worship is not entertainment. It is edification. It is not about creating vibes but about growing in spirit and truth.

In the early church, true worship was centered on prayer, Scripture, and the breaking of bread. It was an act of adoration and submission, rooted in a desire to glorify God and learn from His Word. Early Christian gatherings were about igniting spiritual growth and building up the body of believers, not creating a production.

To return to authentic worship, the church must refocus on Scripture, exalt Christ above all, and resist conforming to the culture of the world. Worship must be rooted in the foundation of God's transformative Word. As Jesus told the Samaritan woman: *God is spirit, and his worshipers must worship in the Spirit and in truth*" (John 4:24). Worship shaped by truth centers on God's revelation of Himself and His redemptive work through Christ.

The Bible emphasizes that true worship transforms us through the power of Scripture. Paul writes in 2 Timothy 3:16-17: *All Scripture is God-breathed and is useful for teaching, rebuking, correcting, and training in righteousness, so that the servant of God may be thoroughly equipped for every good work.* Worship that does not prioritize the Bible fails to fulfill its purpose: to build up believers and point them to Christ. Similarly, in 1 Corinthians 14:26, Paul reminds the church: *Everything must be done so that the church may be built up.* Worship must center on instruction in the Word, strengthening believers in their faith and understanding of the gospel.

Emotions must not overshadow the truth of God's Word. These expressive experiences, though meaningful, are fleeting and often manipulated by external factors like music or performances. However, the truth of Scripture has the power to produce eternal transformation. Worship should engage the heart and mind, leading to genuine growth rather than temporary emotional highs. Theatrics can enthrall but rarely change us. It is often passive, offering a momentary escape without requiring engagement or reflection.

Edification, however, is active. Spiritual enlightenment challenges us to engage with God's truth allowing it to shape our hearts and minds. As Paul writes in Romans 12:2: *Do not conform to the pattern of this world but be transformed by the renewing of your mind.* The church is called to offer something deeper than amusement. It is called to offer the life-changing power of the gospel.

When the church mimics the entertainment-driven mindset of the world, it risks losing its distinct identity and prophetic voice. The focus shifts from holiness to hype, from transformation to tolerance, and from conviction to comfort. But the gospel calls us higher. The church exists to proclaim the truth that sets people free (John 8:32), equip believers for ministry (Ephesians 4:12), and shine as a light in the darkness (Matthew 5:14). The gospel does not need to amuse in order to make it powerful; it is the power of God unto salvation (Romans 1:16).

The church must resist this pull and reclaim its mission of edification. This path may not be easy, but it is faithful. By choosing to instruct in moral and spiritual matters, the church builds worshipers rather than spectators, disciples rather than consumers, and faithful witnesses rather than cultural imitators. The early church thrived not through elaborate productions but through faithful teaching, genuine fellowship, and a commitment to the apostles' doctrine.

We do not need to become more like the world to reach the world. We need to become more like Christ. As Paul reminds us, the church's strength lies not in appealing to societal customs but in proclaiming the truth. The temptation to conform to current culture is strong, but the call to transformation is stronger. The church must remain rooted in the eternal truths of God's Word, not offering the world fleeting pleasures but lasting transformation. When the church chooses faithfulness over spectacle, it fulfills its mission as the body of Christ and shines as a beacon of hope in a world desperate for truth.

Questions

1. What parts of church culture might be hollow hype?

2. How can I avoid going along with trends that value entertainment over truth?

3. Is my worship pleasing to God?

4. Does my church's worship style draw attention to Christ or to the performers?

Ethan

Ethan had always been into music. As a guitarist in his church band, he loved the energy of the services, bright lights, great sound, and songs that really hit home. The church was growing quickly, and Sunday mornings felt more like concerts than regular services. People came from everywhere to soak up the excitement.

But over time, Ethan noticed something off. His friends would rave about how "awesome" the music was or how impressive the stage looked, but they rarely mentioned what they'd learned from the Bible or how their lives were changing. Some even left right after the music, skipping the sermon. It seemed like worship had turned into more of a show instead of focusing on God.

One week, Ethan's home group met at Sarah's place. They talked about "Worship in Spirit and Truth." As they read from Psalms and the New Testament, they reflected on what worship really meant. Sarah said, "Sometimes I think we care more about impressing people than lifting up God. Are we really helping souls, or just entertaining a crowd?"

Ethan felt a pang of guilt. He thought about how much time the band put into nailing songs and coordinating lights, compared to how little time they spent in prayer and getting their hearts ready. He realized it was easy to treat worship like a product and judging it by how it made him feel instead of if it brought him closer to God.

During their talk, an older member, Mr. White, reminisced about quieter church days, "We didn't have fancy gear, but we left changed. Worship was about giving of ourselves, not showcasing a show." The room fell silent as they let that sink in.

Feeling challenged, the group brainstormed ways to get back to genuine worship. They decided to pray more before services, encourage stories of real change, and read more Scripture during worship. Ethan suggested that the band play a simple, acoustic set the following Sunday, inviting the congregation to join in instead of just watching.

That week, the service felt different. The music was simple, the lights were low. The congregation's voices filled the room, creating a deeper sense of reverence. Afterward, several people shared how the focus on God's Word and prayer made worship feel more meaningful. Ethan realized that true growth often happens when performance takes a backseat to God's presence and when worship shifts from what we put on stage to what God does in us.

From then on, the home group kept reminding each other that worship is about transformation, not just entertainment. Their church slowly started changing from a flashy production to a community focused on Christ, eager for the Word and a genuine connection with God.

Cupcakes of Comfort

Ingredients:

- 1 pre-packaged "You Are Enough" mix
- 3 tablespoons of Therapeutic Theology
- 1 scoop of Half-Scripture Filling
- 1 swirl of "Everything Happens for a Reason" icing
- Rainbow Sprinkles of Spiritual Ambiguity

Instructions:

1. Combine the mix with whatever current culture approves.
2. Bake in a pan lined with applause and softened expectations.
3. Ice heavily with emotionalism.
4. Top with sprinkles that look like truth but dissolve quickly.

WARNING LABEL:

Serves: Sunday crowds
Prep Time: 30 minutes or less (No real study required)
Outcome: Satisfied feelings, starved spirit
May look good in Instagram devotionals. Contains no spiritual fiber. Leaves you asking for seconds, but never changes your life.

Chapter 4: Sugar Cookies That Leave a Bitter Taste

Key Verse: Woe to you, teachers of the law and Pharisees, you hypocrites! You clean the outside of the cup and dish, but inside they are full of greed and self-indulgence.

(Matthew 23:25)

In the world of baking, sugar cookies are often seen as a simple, sweet treat. They are easy to make, easy to eat, and always seem to bring a smile to one's face. Yet, despite their popularity, sugar cookies can leave a bitter aftertaste if consumed in excess. They are sweet, but ultimately shallow, offering little more than a temporary sugar rush. For all their appeal, sugar cookies are not the kind of food that nourishes the body. After a few moments of sweetness, the feeling of hunger returns, and something more substantial is craved.

The same can be said of many sermons preached in churches today. Like sugar cookies, some sermons may appear appealing at first, offering sweet, positive messages that make listeners feel good in the moment. They are easy to deliver, easy to hear, and always seem to bring a smile to one's face. These messages might emphasize comfort, encouragement, or motivation. They are sweet, but ultimately shallow, offering little more than a temporary sugar rush. After a few moments of sweetness, the feeling of hunger returns, often accompanied by a sense of disappointment. Without a deeper foundation in the truth of Scripture, they fail to provide the lasting spiritual nourishment and transformation that believers need. Fast food is convenient, but it's not the healthiest option. Like fast food, these messages provide temporary satisfaction but fail to sustain long-term spiritual health.

Scripture repeatedly emphasizes the necessity of spiritual nourishment. In Matthew 4:4, Jesus declares: *Man shall not live on bread alone, but on every word that comes from the mouth of God.* Just as our bodies require solid food to grow and thrive, our souls need the solid truth of Scripture to mature in faith. Similarly, Peter exhorts believers in 1 Peter 2:2: *Like newborn babies, crave pure spiritual milk, so that by it you may grow up in your salvation.* Sugar-coated sermons, like diluted milk, fail to provide the nourishment believers need.

For those seeking to build a life in Christ, quick *spiritual snacks* won't suffice. True discipleship requires the solid, substantial nourishment of God's Word that is capable of sustaining believers through life's difficulties. We cannot overlook the fact that the gospel isn't about personal success but about dying to self, taking up our cross, and following Christ wherever He leads even if it involves suffering, sacrifice, and persecution.

In a world that is filled with pain, hardship, and uncertainty, people crave words of hope and encouragement. The Bible does offer comfort and positivity, but the true comfort of the gospel is not the kind of easy, feel-good positivity that avoids the hard truths of life and faith. True comfort in the gospel comes from the hope of eternal life, the peace of Christ, and the knowledge that even in suffering, God is at work to conform us into the image of His Son.

One hallmark of these glazed messages is it creates congregations that are emotionally stirred but not spiritually reformed. These sermons avoid essential aspects of the Christian life by not confronting sin, repentance, holiness, and discipleship. Many preachers aim to elicit passionate responses through personal stories or motivational messages designed to inspire hope and positivity. While emotions are a natural part of the Christian experience, feelings cannot form the foundation of genuine faith. True faith must be rooted in the eternal truths of God's Word. As the Apostle Paul writes in 1Corinthians 2:4-5: *My message and my preaching were not with wise and persuasive words, but with a demonstration of the Spirit's power, so that your faith might not rest on human wisdom, but on God's power.* These enthusiastic words may inspire temporarily, but only the power of God's truth can produce lasting spiritual conversion to equip believers to face life's trials.

The gospel is not about what we can get from God but about what He has done for us through Jesus Christ. It calls us to repentance, self-denial, and a life of obedience. As Jesus warns in Matthew 23:25: *Woe to you, teachers of the law and Pharisees, you hypocrites! You clean the outside of the cup and dish, but inside they are full of greed and self-indulgence.* In the same way, sugar-coated sermons may focus on outward success and emotional appeal while neglecting the call to inward modification.

The true message of the gospel is that we are sinners in need of redemption and that following Christ requires putting His will and the needs of others above ourselves. Surface-level sermons often avoid these difficult truths, leaving people with a shallow understanding of discipleship. They may uplift temporarily, but they cannot prepare believers to endure trials, resist sin, or grow in holiness.

The antidote to sugar-coated sermons is a return to preaching the whole counsel of God. The gospel is both comforting and challenging, offering the promises of grace alongside the demands of repentance and holiness. As Paul declares in Acts 20:27: *For I have not hesitated to proclaim to you the whole will of God.*

Faithful preaching requires delivering all of Scripture's truths, including the convicting realities of sin and the cost of following Christ. When churches avoid these truths to please the masses, they strip the gospel of its power to change lives. True spiritual growth only happens when God's Word is preached in its fullness.

Paul warns in 2 Timothy 4:3 that: *the time will come when people will not put up with sound doctrine. Instead, to suit their own desires, they will gather around them a great number of teachers to say what their itching ears want to hear.* This danger is evident today as many congregations prefer comfort over conviction and entertainment over edification. However, the church must resist this trend and proclaim the gospel in all its depth and power.

The gospel doesn't just offer temporary encouragement. It provides the profound Word of God that sustains believers through every doubt. Leaders must speak the truth in love, and congregations must hunger for the Bread of Life. Lives will be truly changed only by the power of God's truth working through surrendered hearts.

Questions

1. Am I really living like a disciple should?

2. Am I letting Jesus mold me, or am I holding onto old habits that need to go?

3. What habits can I start to get closer to God?

4. Do I crave God's Word daily, or am I content with occasional spiritual "snacks"?

Daniel

Daniel had a knack for grabbing attention. He could captivate a crowd with his words, light up a stage with his charm, and get people emotional with stories that were both touching and entertaining. A former youth pastor who became a bestselling author and speaker, Daniel was pretty well-known in many Christian communities.

He looked the part too, always in sharp suits, with perfectly groomed hair and a smile that could light up a room. Every time he stood up to speak, he made sure he appeared just right. He was obsessed with how people saw him, constantly checking for applause, likes, shares, and invitations.

His main message was straightforward and crowd-friendly: God wants you to be the best version of you. You are enough. Step into your greatness. People loved it. Churches lined up to book him, and his sermons got shared all over social media with hashtags like #Blessed and #PurposeDriven.

But behind the shiny image and the packed schedule, Daniel started to feel uneasy.

After one huge conference with 3,000 attendees, bright lights, and even fog machines, Daniel headed to the greenroom. While sipping alkaline water, an older man in a plain gray suit approached him, holding a well-worn Bible.

"Son," the man said, "you sure know how to speak."

"Thanks! I try to bring hope," Daniel replied with a smile.

The man nodded. "Hope is good, but truth is better. Hope without truth is like sugar without substance. It gives you a quick high but leaves your soul hungry."

Daniel's smile faded a bit. The man added, "You're giving folks a mirror that flatters them. But the gospel isn't just a mirror, it's also a sword. It cuts. It reveals. It calls people to die to themselves, not just feel better."

Daniel tensed. "Are you saying I'm not preaching the gospel?"

"I'm saying you're preaching part of it," the old man answered. "The comforting part. You've missed the convicting part."

That night, Daniel found it hard to sleep. He tossed and turned, rethinking their talk. Was the man just old-school? Out of touch? Jealous? Deep down, he knew better.

He got up, switched on the light, and looked in the mirror. He saw a successful speaker, a celebrated Christian voice. But that night was different. For the first time in a while, he didn't just check his appearance. He looked into his own eyes and didn't like what he saw.

He saw someone who cared more about pleasing crowds than pleasing Christ. He had been preaching self-improvement instead of self-denial, motivation over transformation, and comfort without the cross.

He opened the Bible in his hotel room to Jesus' words: *If anyone would come after me, let him deny himself and take up his cross daily and follow me* (Luke 9:23). Then he turned to Paul: *I have been crucified with Christ. It is no longer I who live, but Christ who lives in me* (Galatians 2:20). And again to Jesus: N*ot everyone who says to me, 'Lord, Lord, 'will enter the kingdom of heaven... but the one who does the will of my Father* (Matthew 7:21).

He closed the Bible slowly. When was the last time he spoke about repentance? About what it takes to follow Jesus? Had he made fans of Jesus instead of disciples?

That moment changed everything.

In the months that followed, Daniel's message shifted. He got fewer bookings, but his desire for truth grew. He lost some followers but found a deeper passion.

He still preached hope but now it was about hope through the cross, not just feel-good words. He still told people God loved them, but he also explained that love called them to repent, surrender, and be made new, not just improved.

He swapped the flattering mirror for the Word of God, which showed the truth, beautiful and harsh.

Sugarcoated Sermon Swirls

Ingredients:

- 2 cups powdered positivity
- 1 cup syrupy self-affirmation
- ½ tsp Scripture sprinkles (selected)
- 1 stick buttered ego
- 3 tbsp artificial flavor of grace without repentance

Directions:

Whisk all ingredients until fluffy and smooth. Pipe into hearts craving comfort. Avoid heat—truth might melt it.

Serving Note: Melts quickly under conviction.

CHAPTER

5

Chapter 5: The Call to Repentance

Key Verse: Repent, then, and turn to God, so that your sins may be wiped out, that times of refreshing may come from the Lord.

(Acts 3:19)

One of the problems in modern Christianity is the emphasis on God's grace without the corresponding call to repentance.

Grace is beautiful, crucial, and what saves us, not our actions (Ephesians 2:8-9). However, grace is often presented as a feel-good idea without emphasizing the change it demands. In the Bible, grace is not a free pass to continue sinning.

Sin is not just a mistake or a flaw. It's a rebellion against a holy God. Anything we put before God is sin. It breaks our relationship with Him and separates us from the life He offers. Repentance acknowledges the reality of sin and our need for God's forgiveness. It restores our relationship with God and is central to the foundation of faith and building a close relationship with Him.

Repentance is a non-negotiable aspect of the gospel. Without it, there can be no salvation. Jesus Himself warned in Luke 13:3: *Unless you repent, you too will all perish.*

Grace is God's unearned kindness, meant to help us turn away from sin and live a transformed life once we repent. A heart that is truly ready to receive God's grace must repent.

Repentance is recognizing our sinfulness and acknowledging our need for God's forgiveness. It's an honest confrontation with the truth about ourselves and our actions, which leads to a change of heart and mind.

Repentance is a process. While most processes occur over a time, the need for repentance hits us all at once. First, we become aware we've broken God's law. We suddenly stop making excuses for our sins and sinful human nature and become aware of who we are in God's eyes. Then we realize Jesus is the only way to salvation, desperately desire to confess our sins and accept God's gift of love and forgiveness. After we surrender to the Lord, we are so grateful to Him that we want to put our sinful ways behind us and follow His teachings.

One of my sons hit his sister. When his mom demanded an apology, he said, "Sorry that she made me mad enough to do that." That's not repentance.

Sometimes, we do the same with God, saying, "Sorry I messed up, but it's just how I am" or "Everyone else is doing it." Real repentance isn't blame-shifting. It's owning up, turning around, and walking back into God's arms.

The parable of the Prodigal Son (Luke 15:11-32) beautifully illustrates repentance. This tale of a wayward son shows repentance involves a moment of clarity, humility, recognition of one's sin, and a desire to return to the father. After squandering his inheritance, the son recognizes the gravity of his sin and decides to return to his father, saying, "Father, I have sinned against heaven and against you" (Luke 15:18-19). The son does not simply regret his actions because they caused him trouble. He acknowledges that he has sinned against God and his father. The father, seeing him from a distance, runs to embrace him, demonstrating God's heart toward those who truly repent. This parable emphasizes the joy and restoration that come with repentance and the Father's grace in welcoming the lost back home.

True repentance is not just about the consequences of sin but about the realization that sin is an offense against a holy God. It's not a fleeting remorse or an emotional moment. It is a deep, transformation that calls us to turn from sin, embrace God's forgiveness, and walk in newness of life.

Today, repentance is often misunderstood or overlooked, both outside and inside the church. Modern culture, dominated by messages of self-affirmation, happiness, and success views repentance as counterintuitive, uncomfortable, or unnecessary.

People are often told they are perfect as they are, or that their mistakes don't matter as long as they mean well. Churches, too, can shy away from this essential doctrine, favoring feel-good messages over the challenging truth. Yet the Bible presents repentance as a vital part of the Christian faith, an essential step for anyone seeking to know God and experience His salvation.

The call to repentance is not a New Testament idea alone. It is deeply rooted in the Old Testament. The Hebrew word for repentance, *shuv,* means to return or turn back. It reflects a call to return to God after going astray, to turn from idolatry and sin, and to renew a relationship with Him.

The prophets repeatedly called Israel to repentance, as seen in Joel 2:12-13: *Even now, declares the Lord, return to me with all your heart, with fasting and weeping and mourning. Rend your heart and not your garments. Return to the Lord your God, for He is gracious and compassionate, slow to anger and abounding in love.* True repentance is not about outward rituals or displays of remorse but a genuine transformation of our heart turning back to God.

Ezekiel echoes this in his plea: *Repent! Turn away from all your offenses; then sin will not be your downfall* (Ezekiel 18:30). Repentance involves both turning away from sin and committing to live in obedience to God. It is how individuals and nations experience forgiveness and restoration.

Repentance remains central in the New Testament. John the Baptist, the forerunner of Jesus, preached repentance to prepare hearts for the Messiah: *Repent, for the kingdom of heaven has come near* (Matthew 3:2). Jesus, too, began His ministry with the same message (Matthew 4:17). The gospel of repentance is not one of condemnation but an invitation to turn to God and experience His mercy and grace.

The apostle Peter underscores the importance of repentance in Acts 2:38: *Repent and be baptized, every one of you, in the name of Jesus Christ for the forgiveness of your sins.*

As Paul writes in 2 Corinthians 7:10: *Godly sorrow brings repentance that leads to salvation and leaves no regret, but worldly sorrow brings death.* Godly sorrow recognizes sin's seriousness and leads to genuine transformation, not just regret over consequences.

Repentance involves sorrow over sin and a decision to change direction. It is not enough to feel bad about one's actions. True repentance requires reorienting priorities, desires, and actions toward God.

Paul makes this clear in Romans 6:1-2: *What shall we say then? Shall we go on sinning so that grace may increase? By no means! We are those who have died to sin; how can we live in it any longer?*

Repentance is the first step toward forgiveness and reconciliation with God. It is also an ongoing process in the believer's life.

While repentance begins with an initial act of turning to God for salvation, it continues throughout the Christian journey. Jesus, in Revelation 3:19, tells the church in Laodicea: *Those whom I love I rebuke and discipline. So be earnest and repent.* Repentance is a lifelong attitude of turning from sin and toward God daily.

This continual turning away from sin and toward God is essential for spiritual growth.

Jesus linked grace to change. He forgave sinners but also urged them to reform. When He told the woman caught in adultery, "Neither do I condemn you," He added, "Go now and leave your life of sin" (John 8:11).

Similarly, Peter's words in Acts 3:19 encapsulate the message of repentance: *Repent, then, and turn to God, so that your sins may be wiped out, that times of refreshing may come from the Lord.* Repentance is not merely an emotional experience but a course change. It reorients our priorities, desires, and actions.

Repentance is not optional in the Christian life. It is the gateway to salvation and spiritual renewal. It is the door through which we experience forgiveness, cleansing, and transformation.

Unfortunately, many churches today preach grace as if it covers sin without the need for repentance. When grace is preached without repentance, it misleads people into thinking they are saved while still living in rebellion against God. Jesus warned in (Matthew 7:21) that: *not everyone who calls Him*

'Lord' will enter heaven, but only those who do the Father's will.

The truth is Jesus loves people as they are but the message often stops there, neglecting the call to turn from sin and grow through the Holy Spirit's power. True grace doesn't leave us in our sin. It pulls us out of darkness into God's light (1 Peter 2:9): *But you are a chosen people, a royal priesthood, a holy nation, God's special possession, that you may declare the praises of him who called you out of darkness into his wonderful light.* Repentance empowers us to live a new life.

The full gospel is a message that presents grace not as permission to sin but as God's power to live rightly. Jesus' death on the cross was the cost for our grace and calls us to give our lives in response. Repentance is not an outdated concept but a transformative process that touches every aspect of a believer's life. It calls for us to turn from sin, embrace God's forgiveness, and walk in newness of life. Anything less leaves people trapped in sin rather than setting them free.

Questions

1. What am I holding onto that keeps me from surrendering my life to Jesus?

2. What does true repentance look like in my life?

3. Have I really turned away from sin, or am I still stuck in bad habits?

4. Do I see my sin the way God sees it, or do I still minimize or excuse it?

Marcus

It was a gloomy Sunday morning. Rain was coming down on the windshield as Marcus sat by himself in his car in the church parking lot. He was super early. The doors weren't even open. So, he leaned back in his seat, checked his phone, and started a Christian radio app.

A well-known pastor's voice came on, all smooth and hyped up. The sermon was already going. "God isn't mad. He totally loves you! You don't have to change to come to Him; just trust He has a great future planned!"

Marcus listened. The pastor quoted some verses about blessings and good fortune. The message was all about being positive. "God wants to take you higher!" "Your big breakthrough is right around the corner!" "Say it, believe it, get it!"

It was the kind of stuff that sounded good at first, but as Marcus watched the rain, he just felt empty.

The words were nice, but he still felt uneasy. "Is that all there is?" he wondered. "What about the stuff I'm struggling with? The guilt I feel? The stuff I know I have to fix?" He shut off the radio.

For weeks, Marcus had been living a fake life. Church on Sundays but doing wrong things the rest of the week. Secret sins. Anger he wouldn't let go of. Stuff he'd been hiding, thinking, "God gets it," and, "grace covers everything."

But today, something was different. The sermon didn't make him feel better. It made him feel worse. Not because it called out his sin, but because it didn't even mention it. He opened his Bible app and searched 'Repent'. "*Repent, because the kingdom of heaven is near*" (Matthew 3:2). *If you don't turn away from your sins, you will all be destroyed* (Luke 13:3). *Godly sorrow makes us turn away from sin, which leads to salvation* (2 Corinthians 7:10).

That word kept popping up: repent. And it clicked.

It wasn't just about feeling bad. It wasn't about saying sorry and then going back to the same old stuff. Repentance was a call to change. To go in a new direction. To give up. Not just his bad habits, but everything.

Marcus put his head on the steering wheel, crying as he listened to the rain. "I've been trying to feel good, Lord, but I need to be cleaned up. I've been avoiding what I know is right, but I need to be changed. I'm sorry. I repent. Make me new."

Marshmallow Message Squares

Ingredients:

- 3 cups puffy promises
- 1 bag melted "you do you" doctrine
- ½ cup marshmallow self-worth
- 1 tsp reduced sin extract
- ¼ cup candy-coated clichés

Instructions:

Press mixture into a shallow pan of low expectations. Chill in a culture of compromise.

Warning: May cause spiritual cavities.

CHAPTER

6

Chapter 6: Dying to Self

Key Verse: I have been crucified with Christ and I no longer live, but Christ lives in me.

(Galatians 2:20)

Dying to self is often a misunderstood part of the Christian journey, but it is fundamental to discipleship. It's not about making a one-time decision. It's something we work on every day. It affects all areas of our lives through our thoughts, wants, actions, and relationships. Paul captures this truth in Galatians 2:20: *I have been crucified with Christ and I no longer live, but Christ lives in me.*

Though dying to self is challenging, it also brings incredible blessings. When we surrender our lives to Christ and die to our own desires, we experience a deeper, more fulfilling life than we could have ever imagined on our own.

To die to self means to relinquish our personal wants and ambitions to align with God's purposes. In other words, to surrender every aspect of life to Him and allow Him to take control and reshape us into His image. It's not about hating ourselves or feeling worthless. It's about letting go of self-centeredness to embrace the fuller life that comes from submitting fully to Christ. True surrender to Christ allows us to evolve day-by-day.

The Christian life is full of paradoxes. At its heart is the truth that to find life we must first lose it. Jesus declared in Matthew 16:25: *For whoever wants to save their life will lose it, but whoever loses their life for me will find it.* It is not just a theological idea but a practical reality every follower of Jesus must live out.

The call to die to self is rooted in Jesus Christ's example. His entire life was marked by self-sacrifice, humility, and surrender to God's will. From His birth to His death on the cross, Jesus demonstrated what it means to live fully for God. Philippians 2:5-8 describes His humility: *In your relationships with one another, have the same mindset as Christ Jesus: Who, being in very nature God, did not consider equality with God something to be used to His own advantage; rather, He made Himself nothing by taking the very nature of a servant, being made in human likeness. And being found in appearance as a man, He humbled Himself by becoming obedient to death. Even death on a cross!*

Jesus, the eternal Son of God, humbled Himself to take on human flesh and, ultimately, to die on the cross for the sins of man. His life and death were the ultimate example of dying to self. He lived not for His own comfort or glory but for the glory of the Father and the salvation of humanity. His prayer in Gethsemane encapsulates the heart of self-denial and surrender: *Father, if you are willing, take this cup from me; yet not my will, but yours be done* (Luke 22:42).

Jesus calls His followers to the same path of surrender. In Matthew 16:24, He says: *Whoever wants to be my disciple must deny themselves and take up their cross and follow me.*

The cross was not just a symbol of suffering but a symbol of death. A death to self, pride, and earthly aspirations. Daily. To live for Him.

Dying to self was not abstract to Paul. It was a lived experience. In Romans 6:6, he writes: *Our old self was crucified with Him so that the body ruled by sin might be done away with, that we should no longer be slaves to sin.* His old ambitions and desires were replaced with a singular focus on glorifying Christ. This radical conversion was the foundation of his faith and ministry.

When we die to self, we reorder our priorities. Paul speaks of this change in Philippians 3:7-8: *Whatever were gains to me I now consider loss for the sake of Christ. What is more, I consider everything a loss because of the surpassing worth of knowing Christ Jesus my Lord, for whose sake I have lost all things. I consider them garbage, that I may gain Christ.*

Before encountering Christ, Paul's life was centered on his achievements and status. Afterward, he realized these were worthless compared to knowing Christ. To die to self means letting go of personal motivations and embracing our new identity in Him. Our pursuit of wealth, status, power, and even personal happiness must take a backseat to our pursuit of God's kingdom and His righteousness.

This shift in priorities also transforms our relationships. Jesus says in Matthew 10:37: *Anyone who loves their father or mother more than me is not worthy of me; anyone who loves their son or daughter more than me is not worthy of me.* This verse doesn't mean we should treat our family with disrespect. Exodus 20:12 tells us to: *Honor your father and mother.* Matthew 10:37 means: Our love for Christ must surpass even our closest earthly relationships. Dying to self means placing Christ above all else.

At its core, dying to self is about surrendering our will to God's. The heart of sin is the yearning to assert our will over His. From the beginning, humanity's rebellion in the Garden of Eden stemmed from choosing our way over God's. To die to self is to reverse this rebellion and submit fully to God's will. Remember Jesus' prayer in Gethsemane in Luke 22:42? Even though Jesus knew the suffering He would endure on the cross, He submitted His will to God. This act of surrender was the ultimate act of dying to self.

Romans 12:1-2 urges believers to *offer their bodies as living sacrifices, holy and pleasing to God.* This act of surrender touches every area of life. It requires trusting that God's will is better than our own.

Jesus' call to take up our cross daily (Luke 9:23) reminds us that this is an ongoing journey. Each day, we must choose to reject sin and live in obedience to Christ. Paul writes in 2 Corinthians 4:11: *For we who are alive are always being given over to death for Jesus' sake, so that His life may also be revealed in our mortal body.* This continual dying to sin, self, and the world is the path to experiencing the fullness of life in Him.

Our ultimate goal is to surrender our lives to Christ, thereby, allowing Him to make us into His likeness. The more we die to self, the more Christ can live through us. We become conformed to His image and His character is developed in us. This is the process of sanctification and being made holy and Christ-like.

In Colossians 3:9-10, Paul writes: *You have taken off your old self with its practices and have put on the new self, which is being renewed in knowledge in the image of its Creator.* This reconstruction is not superficial but a complete renewal of who we are. As we die to self, the Holy Spirit shapes us to be more Christ-like, producing His character in us.

One of the clearest indicators that we are dying to self and being rebuilt into the image of Christ is the fruit of the Spirit: *Love, joy, peace, forbearance, kindness, goodness, faithfulness, gentleness, and self-control* (Galatians 5:22-23). These traits reflect Christ's character. They grow in us as we surrender to Him. This transformation is not something we achieve on our own but is the result of the Holy Spirit working within us.

Sacrificial love is one of the signs of dying to self. Jesus demonstrated the ultimate act of love when He laid down His life for us. In John 15:13, He says: *Greater love has no one than this: to lay down one's life for one's friends.* Dying to self enables us to love others with the same selflessness and compassion. This might mean forgiving those who hurt us, putting others' needs before our own, or serving those in need. Sacrificial love reflects Christ's love and is the fruit of a life surrendered to Him.

Jesus says in Matthew 6:33: *Seek first His kingdom and His righteousness, and all these things will be given to you as well.* Before all else, we must prioritize God's kingdom above our own desires. We live for His glory, using our time, talents, and resources to serve Him and advance His mission.

The lifelong process of dying to self leads to a deeper intimacy with Christ, greater peace and joy, and freedom from sin's power. As we surrender more of ourselves to Christ, we discover the abundant life Christ offers, filled with His presence, love, and objective. Becoming more like Him.

May we embrace this call to die to self, allowing Christ to transform us into His image for His glory and live lives that reflect His love, grace, and truth to the world. Though the cost of discipleship is high, the eternal rewards far outweigh the sacrifice.

Questions

1. What does it mean to lose my life for Christ?

2. How am I giving up my own plans to live for God's purposes?

3. How do I live out the truth that I am crucified with Christ?

Evelyn

Evelyn stood in front of her bathroom mirror. Her makeup was half done, and her hair was in a messy bun. She'd even left a hot curling iron sitting out. She'd just ended a phone call after having another disturbing fight with her sister. Evelyn had been super defensive, using sharp words and refusing to say sorry. Now, staring at her reflection, she felt haunted by her own bad mood.

In that quiet moment, she started thinking about a church service from months ago. A friend had invited her to some trendy church downtown. She remembered the good vibes, the cool atmosphere, and especially what the pastor said.

He'd said, "God wants you to enjoy life now. You're good enough. Just be yourself, and God will make it work."

Everyone clapped. Evelyn too. It sounded good, like she was getting permission to go after her dreams without feeling bad, to put herself first, to protect her space.

But today that message felt fake.

Her enjoyable life still felt like a mess. Her relationships were a struggle. Her spiritual life was boring. And just being herself had made her more selfish, more defensive, and just plain tired.

She grabbed her Bible, which had been sitting on a shelf collecting dust. Not knowing where to start, she just opened it randomly and landed in Luke. *If anyone wants to follow me, they must say no to themselves. They must pick up their cross every day and follow me* (Luke 9:23).

Those words hit hard. Say no to yourself. Pick up your cross. Follow Me. This wasn't the sweet stuff she remembered from that sermon. This was real, and it hurt.

Evelyn got it. The gospel she'd believed in was all about her. Her goals. Her feelings Her happiness. But Jesus was asking her to do more. Not to hate herself. To let go of the version of herself that didn't involve Him.

Her stubbornness on that phone call? Her big head? Her not wanting to forgive? That was the self Jesus wanted her to get rid of.

She sat down on the edge of the bathtub and whispered, tears in her eyes: Jesus I've been holding on so tight to myself. My rights, how I look, being in control. But I'm empty. I need You. Help me say goodbye to this old self and live for You.

Selfie Sundae Gospel

Ingredients:

- 1 scoop spiritual self-help
- 2 scoops feel-good faith
- Whipped dreams
- Cherry-picked verses
- Rainbow sprinkles of vague hope

Instructions:

Layer your preferences. Top with syrupy sayings. Ignore sin, repentance, and sacrifice.

Best enjoyed: Solo. No sharing required.

Chapter 7: The True Gospel

Key Verse: Go therefore and make disciples of all nations, baptizing them in the name of the Father and of the Son and of the Holy Spirit.

(Matthew 28:19)

Defining *the true gospel* is essential to understanding what it means to follow Jesus. It is not just about admiring Him or showing up at church. It's about changing our life and making disciples. This message shapes how we view salvation and how we live out our faith day-by-day.

The gospel of Jesus Christ is the key message of Christianity. Yet, in today's world, it is often diluted, misrepresented, or ignored.

What is the true gospel? What does it mean to follow Jesus? And how can we distinguish the true gospel from the false gospels around us?

At its core, the gospel is the good news of God's salvation through Jesus Christ. It proclaims that God, in His great mercy, has made a way for sinful humanity to be reconciled, to re-establish a relationship, with Him through the life, death, and resurrection of Jesus. This good news is not just about the promise of eternal life. It is also about the transformation of our hearts and lives in the present. The gospel is the power of God to save, redeem, and restore, forming the foundation for all Christian life and practice.

However, the Word of God is often reduced to a simplified message: *Jesus died for your sins so you can go to heaven.* While factual, this principle neglects the full depth of the gospel, which calls individuals not only to believe theological truths but to also become active participants in God's kingdom. God demands transformed lives and genuine discipleship.

The true gospel is about more than individual salvation. It involves the restoration of all things. In Romans 8:19-22, Paul writes about the groaning of creation as it waits for redemption: *For the creation waits in eager expectation for the children of God to be revealed. For the creation was subjected to frustration, not by its own choice, but by the will of the one who subjected it, in hope that the creation itself will be liberated from its bondage to decay and brought into the freedom and glory of the children of God. We know that the whole creation has been groaning as in the pains of childbirth right up to the present time.* The gospel is God's plan not just to save people but to redeem all creation, restoring the world to its original perfection and glory.

The word *gospel* originates from the Greek word *euangelion*, meaning *good news* or *glad tidings*. In the New Testament, it refers to the message of salvation through Jesus Christ. It is the announcement of what God accomplished for us that we could not accomplish for ourselves. As Paul declares in Romans 1:16: *For I am not ashamed of the gospel because it is the power of God that brings salvation to everyone who believes: first to the Jew, then to the Gentile.* The gospel is not just a set of ideas. It is the very power of God to bring salvation by grace.

God's good news begins with the reality of human sinfulness. The Bible teaches that: *all have sinned and fall short of the glory of God* (Romans 3:23). Sin is not just about individual acts of wrongdoing. It represents the condition of the human heart and our separation from God. Because of sin, we deserve God's judgment and eternal separation. Yet the gospel proclaims the good news that God, in His love, sent His Son to take the penalty for our sin. As John 3:16 says: *For God so loved the world that He gave His one and only Son, that whoever believes in Him shall not perish but have eternal life.*

Through His death and resurrection, Jesus conquered sin and death, offering forgiveness and reconciliation with God. This gospel is not only about future hope in heaven but also about the present reality of God's kingdom infiltrating our lives. Jesus proclaimed in Mark 1:15: *The kingdom of God has come near. Repent and believe the good news!* The gospel invites us to live under God's reign today, following His teachings and participating in His mission.

This message radically changes individuals. When we place our faith in Jesus, we are not only forgiven but are made new. As Paul writes in 2 Corinthians 5:17: *If anyone is in Christ, the new creation has come: The old has gone, the new is here!* The gospel brings inner transformation, as the Holy Spirit works to make us more like Christ, shifting our priorities, desires, attitudes, and actions.

While many people may accept the gospel message in a moment of emotional response from a euphoric sugar-coated message, the Bible calls people to something deeper; discipleship. Jesus said in Matthew 4:19: *Come, follow me, and I will send you out to fish for people.* Discipleship involves following Jesus wherever He leads, learning from Him, imitating Him, and sharing His message. It means embracing His mission and living under His Lordship.

True discipleship is about conversion and obedience. In Matthew 28:20, Jesus emphasizes teaching disciples to obey His commands. Discipleship is not merely about knowledge but about living in alignment with God's Word. James 1:22 reminds us: *Do not merely listen to the word and so deceive yourselves. Do what it says.*

Living as a disciple of Jesus comes with a cost. Jesus warned in Luke 14:27: *Whoever does not carry their cross and follow me cannot be my disciple.* Following Jesus may involve suffering, rejection, and sacrifice. But it is a commitment worth making because of the eternal life, joy, and purpose it brings. Jesus compares discipleship to building a tower or going to war, both of which require careful planning and counting the cost. To be a devoted disciple of Jesus is to commit to Him wholeheartedly, without reserve, and to be willing to give up everything for the sake of His kingdom.

Discipleship is not only about personal growth. The ultimate goal of discipleship is multiplication. It is about making disciples who make disciples. Disciples making disciples who make disciples is how the gospel spread through the early church and continues to spread today.

In the Great Commission, Jesus commands: *Go and make disciples of all nations, baptizing them in the name of the Father and of the Son and of the Holy Spirit, and teaching them to obey everything I have commanded you* (Matthew 28:19-20). This mission is not optional. It is the very purpose of the church. Discipleship requires nurturing others in their faith, teaching them to obey Jesus, and helping them to grow in their relationship with God. As Paul instructed Timothy in 2 Timothy 2:2: *The things you have heard me say in the presence of many witnesses entrust to reliable people who will also be qualified to teach others.* Discipleship is not about creating dependence on a teacher but about equipping others to grow in faith and make disciples themselves.

Likewise, the church plays a vital role in discipleship. The church body is the community where believers are equipped, supported, and encouraged to grow in their faith. Paul writes in Ephesians 4:11-13: *So Christ himself gave the apostles, the prophets, the evangelists, the pastors and teachers, to equip his people for works of service, so that the body of Christ may be built up until we all reach unity in the faith and in the knowledge of the Son of God and become mature, attaining to the whole measure of the fullness of Christ.* Discipleship thrives when one is in association with like-minded believers who hold one another accountable, share life together, and encourage each other's spiritual growth.

Discipleship is not always convenient or easy. It requires time, energy, and intentional investment in others. It means walking alongside people in their spiritual journeys, encouraging them, teaching them, and at times lovingly challenging them. Jesus modeled this with His disciples, spending three years teaching them, correcting them, and showing them how to live according to God's kingdom. In John 15:8, He says: *This is to my Father's glory, that you bear much fruit, showing yourselves to be my disciples.* The fruit that Jesus desires from us is a life of obedience to Him and the making of other disciples.

Evangelism and discipleship go hand in hand. While evangelism introduces people to Christ, discipleship nurtures them in their faith and equips them to live as Christ's followers. Evangelism without discipleship leads to shallow conversions, while discipleship without evangelism fails to fulfill the Great Commission. Both are essential, but discipleship is the ultimate goal.

Jesus said in Matthew 6:33: *Seek first His kingdom and His righteousness.* When disciples live out the gospel, they bring God's light and love into every part of life such as workplaces, schools, neighborhoods, and governments. The kingdom of God grows as disciples make disciples, transforming lives and communities.

The true gospel is not just information to believe. It is a call to renewal and pursuing a mission. It is the glad tidings of God's salvation, the restoration of all things, and the invitation to follow Jesus daily. May we embrace this gospel fully, becoming disciples who live for Christ and make Him known to the world.

Questions

1. How is God changing me?

2. Am I truly a disciple of Christ?

3. In what ways am I actively making disciples, not just attending church?

4. Who am I intentionally investing in to help them grow in their faith?

5. Would others recognize me as a disciple of Jesus by the fruit in my life?

Jason

The coffee shop buzzed on a regular Tuesday morning. The smell of a fresh brew permeated the room as Jason sat down across from Bryan, his old buddy from college.

They hadn't seen each other in ages, so catching up was a must.

Bryan took a sip and smiled. "So, how's church? Still at that big one on the west side?"

Jason nodded. "Yep, same place. I dig it. It's super positive, the music rocks, and the sermons are chill and encouraging. I need that with everything going on, to be honest."

Bryan leaned back, "I feel you. But does it ever feel like it's enough? Like, you just go, hear a sermon, feel good, and then head home?".

Jason rubs his chin. "What do you mean?"

Bryan hesitated, then leaned in. "I've been struggling with what it really means to follow Jesus. Not just believe or go to church but actually follow."

Jason blinked. "Isn't that the same thing?"

Bryan shook his head. "I used to think so, too. But I've been reading the Gospels again, and Jesus didn't say, 'Admire me from a distance.' He said, 'Pick up your cross and follow me.' He didn't just want people to show up, He wanted them to become disciples."

Jason leaned in. "So what's the difference?"

Bryan took a breath. "The more I look at it, the more I see that the gospel isn't just about going to heaven when we die. It's about Jesus being King right now, and us giving him every part of our lives."

Jason nodded slowly.

Bryan kept going, "The real gospel doesn't just say, 'Believe and you will be blessed.' It says, 'Turn from your sins and let God change you.' It's not just an invite to have your sins forgiven, it's a call to totally change."

"See," Bryan added, "Jesus didn't die just to make us feel better, He died to make us new. New hearts, new desires, new lives. And He didn't just call us to be saved, He called us to make disciples, not fans."

Jason frowned. "But isn't everyone who believes a disciple?"

Bryan smiled gently. "Not really. Think of it like this, Jesus had tons of followers. They loved the miracles, the healings, the free food. But when He started talking about sacrifice, suffering, and obeying… most of them left."

Jason looked out the window, thinking hard. "So… you're saying I've been more like a fan?"

Bryan didn't answer for a moment. "I think a lot of us have man. I know I have. But Jesus didn't say, 'If you feel like it, try Me out.' He said, 'Forget yourself, pick up your cross every day, and follow Me.' That's not an easy message; that's a call to give up on yourself."

Jason sat back. "That's kind of intense, to be honest."

"It is," Bryan agreed. "But it's also freeing. Because when we give him everything like our jobs, relationships, time, money, even our dreams, that's when we find real life. That's when Jesus becomes more than just a Sunday thing. He becomes the boss of our lives."

Jason looked up. "So, what does that mean for you now?"

"Well," Bryan said, "I stopped asking what I could get from church and started asking who I could help. I got a mentor and started teaching a younger believer. It's not about me anymore, it's about sharing Jesus with others."

Jason sighed. "Wow. That's... different. But kind of cool."

Bryan smiled. "It's not a walk in the park. But it's worth it. That's what Jesus meant when He said, 'Go and make disciples of all nations. He didn't say go build up crowds. He said go build up people."

As their coffee got cold and the conversation got deep, Jason started wondering if his faith had been lazy. Was it about feeling good, staying comfy, and just taking things in... instead of really following?

Bryan leaned in one last time. "The real gospel? It's not always nice. It hits you with your sins, wants you to give up control, and tells you to obey. But it also gives you joy, peace, purpose, and a life that no easy message can ever give."

Jason nodded slowly, his heart moved. "Okay. So where do I even start?"

Bryan grinned. "You already did. You asked the question. Now you must think about what it will cost and follow."

Vanilla Vision Cupcakes

Ingredients:

- 1½ cups fluffy vision statements
- ½ cup light theology
- 3 tbsp sugar substitute (truth-free)
- 1 tub frosting of endless blessings

Directions:

Bake just long enough to draw a crowd. Avoid bold spices like correction or conviction.

Pairs well with: Trendy branding and fog machines.

CHAPTER 8

Chapter 8: Sacrificial Living

Key Verse: Therefore, I urge you, brothers and sisters, in view of God's mercy, to offer your bodies as a living sacrifice, holy and pleasing to God, this is your true and proper worship.

(Romans 12:1)

Sacrificial Living defines the Christian life. Every day we must choose God's will over our own desires, His kingdom over our gain, and His purpose over our plans.

The Bible calls believers to give themselves fully to God and not as a mere ritual or ceremony but as a daily act of devotion. As Paul writes in Romans 12:1: *Offer your bodies as a living sacrifice, holy and pleasing to God, this is your true and proper worship.* Living sacrificially means surrendering every part of our lives to God, not out of guilt or duty, but in response to His mercy and grace. This involves surrendering our heart, mind, and body into His hands, allowing Him to guide our lives for His purpose rather than our own. Scripture provides countless examples of this submitted lifestyle, which transforms us and leads to a life centered on God.

Throughout history some of the most profound expressions of love and devotion have come from those who chose to live sacrificially. These are the people who, in response to God's love and mercy, offer their lives fully, without reservation, for His purposes. Sacrificial living is not about doing something out of obligation. It is a response to God's overwhelming grace. A willingness to give up personal comfort, security, and pride for the glory of God. It is living with a radical sense of purpose, fully surrendered to God's will, and seeing every moment as an opportunity to serve Him.

The story of the Woman with the Alabaster Jar in Matthew 26:7 is a beautiful example of love and sacrifice. A woman came to Jesus with an alabaster jar of a lavish, expensive perfume and poured it on His head as he reclined at the table. This perfume was likely the most valuable thing she owned, but she gave it all to honor Jesus. It was her way of showing deep love and preparing Him for what was to come. Jesus praised her saying that her story would be told for all time. So next time you have a chance to show love through sacrificial giving, think of the woman who poured out her best for Jesus.

The story of the Widow of Zarephath shows the power of sacrificial love and faith in God. Even though she was very poor and had only one meal left, she chose to share it with the prophet Elijah. She trusted God's promise, and because of her faith, God made sure her jar of flour was not used up, and her jug of oil did not run dry, in keeping with the word of the Lord spoken by Elijah (1 Kings 17:8-16). Her willing compliance reminds us that even in hard times trusting God and giving our all can lead to great blessings.

The world encourages us to accumulate wealth for ourselves, but Jesus teaches us to store up treasures in heaven (Matthew 6:19-21). Sacrificial living involves giving generously, not only when convenient but as an act of worship. Whether supporting the poor, furthering the gospel, or meeting others' needs, sacrificial giving reflects our trust in God as our provider.

Abraham's story is one of the strongest examples of faith and sacrifice in the Bible. God tested Abraham by asking him to sacrifice his son Isaac. In Genesis 22:2: *Then God said, take your son, your only son whom you love, Isaac, and go to the region of Moriah, sacrifice him there as a burnt offering on a mountain that I will show you.* Even though it must have been heartbreaking and confusing for him to offer up the son God had promised him, Abraham obeyed without delay.

Abraham got up early, prepared for the journey, and took Isaac to the mountain. When Isaac noticed there was no lamb for the offering, Abraham said with faith, "God will provide the lamb." Abraham believed that even if he had to sacrifice Isaac, God could bring him back to life (Hebrews 11:17–19). Just as Abraham is about to fulfill God's request, an angel stopped him and told him not to harm Isaac. God then provided a ram to take Isaac's place.

God blessed Abraham greatly for his faith and obedience by promising that his descendants would be as many as the stars in the sky and sand on the seashore (Genesis 22:16–17).

Abraham's faithful act demonstrates such a strong trust in God that he obeyed even when it was emotionally crushing. Like Abraham, we are called to live a life of sacrifice, trusting God fully and not holding anything back from Him.

The ultimate example of sacrificial living is found in Jesus Christ. Philippians 2:5-8 describes His humility: *In your relationships with one another, have the same mindset as Christ Jesus: Who, being in very nature God, did not consider equality with God something to be used to His own advantage; rather, He made Himself nothing by taking the very nature of a servant, being made in human likeness. And being found in appearance as a man, He humbled Himself by becoming obedient to death, even death on a cross!*

God's plan of redemption was fulfilled when Jesus sacrificed His comfort, reputation, and life for us. Christ demonstrated ultimate obedience, humility, and selflessness on the cross. To follow Him, we must adopt the same mindset, surrendering our own ambitions and desires to serve others and glorify God. We are called to follow His example in our relationships by putting others' needs before our own, forgiving, and loving unconditionally.

However, sacrificial living is not about deprivation or suffering for its own sake. It is about finding joy in God. The world seeks fulfillment in pleasure, success, and self-centered living, but Jesus offers a better path. As He says in Matthew 16:25: *Whoever wants to save their life will lose it, but whoever loses their life for me will find it.* True joy comes through sacrificial love and devotion to God, where we discover a deeper sense of purpose and fulfillment.

In Romans, Paul spends the first eleven chapters expounding on the gospel: humanity's sin, justification by faith, God's gift of salvation, and the hope of glory in Christ. Then, in Romans 12:1, he transitions from doctrine to practical living, urging believers to respond to God's mercy with lives of worship. This mercy becomes the foundation and motivation for sacrificial living.

The phrase *living sacrifice* is striking. In the Old Testament, sacrifices involved the death of an animal, offered for atonement or worship. But Paul calls for a life fully devoted to God's glory as a *living sacrifice*. This image challenges believers to surrender not just parts of their lives but their whole selves. Being a living sacrifice is not about occasional acts of service or devotion. It is about dedicating every aspect of life to God's purposes as an act of worship. Our bodies, as temples of the Holy Spirit (1 Corinthians 6:19), are to be used for holiness and righteousness, not sinful pleasures or selfish gain. Sacrificial living requires discipline in how we care for and use our bodies to glorify God. It begins with inner transformation not just external acts. Paul continues in Romans 12:2: *Do not conform to the pattern of this world but be transformed by the renewing of your mind.*

True sacrifice involves a complete renewal of our thoughts, desires, and priorities. As we surrender to God, the Holy Spirit works within us, reshaping us to see the world as God does and empowering us to live for His purposes.

A sacrificial life calls us to use our most precious

resource: time. Instead of wasting time on fleeting pleasures, we should invest it in eternal objectives, such as serving others, evangelizing, discipling, and spending time in prayer and worship. Whether teaching, preaching, music, art, or any other skill, each believer is uniquely gifted by God to use those talents to serve others and advance God's kingdom.

Living sacrificially is not easy. It challenges the values of the world and our own selfish desires. It requires discipline and perseverance, and it often involves suffering. But Paul reminds us in Romans 8:18: *I consider that our present sufferings are not worth comparing with the glory that will be revealed in us.* Temporary trials refine our character, strengthen our faith, and prepare us for eternal glory.

A sacrificial lifestyle is not limited to extraordinary acts but is reflected in daily choices. It means laying aside personal agendas to serve others, offering forgiveness, and living with integrity. It is a life of consistent, Christ-like love toward family, friends, and even strangers. As Paul encourages in Ephesians 5:1-2: *Follow God's example, therefore, as dearly loved children and walk in the way of love, just as Christ loved us and gave Himself up for us as a fragrant offering and sacrifice to God.*

Sacrificial living thrives in community. The church is called to reflect Christ's love by serving one another with benevolence and meeting the needs of others. As Jesus said in John 13:35: *By this everyone will know that you are my disciples, if you love one another.* The church becomes a beacon of hope to the world and demonstrates the power of the gospel when they radiate love.

While sacrificial living is challenging, it brings immeasurable rewards. Paul writes in 2 Corinthians 4:17-18: *For our light and momentary troubles are achieving for us an eternal glory that far outweighs them all.* The rewards are not always immediate or material, but they are eternal. Our intimacy deepens with God as we are prepared to share in Christ's eternal joy and glory.

Ultimately, sacrificial living allows us to be a witness to the world. By surrendering our lives to God, we show others the transformative power of the gospel. Our sacrifices point to Jesus, who gave everything for us, and invite others to experience His love and redemption. Sacrificial living is not about loss. It's about gaining a deeper relationship with God and fulfilling His purposes.

May we have the courage to embrace this call, trusting that as we live sacrificially, we walk in the footsteps of Jesus and glorify God with our lives.

Questions

1. Am I really living like a disciple should?

2. What have I given up to follow Jesus?

3. How am I learning, and how am I teaching others to follow Christ better?

Michael

Michael had a good life. He lived in a nice suburb with his wife and two kids, balancing family, work, and faith pretty well. He went to church regularly, gave money to the church, and even volunteered in the parking lot once a month. Life felt safe and stable.

One Sunday, a missionary named Samuel visited the church. He had spent over ten years in a remote area of Southeast Asia. Michael noticed that Samuel didn't have any flashy stories. He was just humble and spoke with a calm but urgent sincerity.

Samuel shared stories about walking long distances through jungles to reach villages that had no electricity but were full of open hearts. He talked about people who had been hurt by religion but found hope in straightforward messages about Jesus. He spoke about tough times not as barriers, but as part of living for Christ.

Then Samuel said something that really hit Michael hard. "Worship isn't just a song on Sunday, it's about surrendering on Monday. True worship means giving yourself completely to God. It's not always easy, but that's where real change happens."

After the service, Michael felt the urge to talk to Samuel. It was as if something inside him was pushing him forward, even though he wasn't quite sure why.

When it was his turn, he introduced himself and said, "Your message really made me think. But I don't even know how to begin living like that. I have a family, a mortgage, a job. I want to live more for others, but I'm not sure what that means for me."

Samuel smiled as if he had heard this before. "Living sacrificially doesn't mean you have to quit everything. Sometimes, it's about giving everything over.

The real question is: *Have I let Jesus into every part of my life, my time, my money, my dreams, my comfort?* Start small. Ask yourself: *Where do I still want control? What am I afraid to give up? What chances to help am I ignoring because they seem too hard?*

That night, Michael couldn't sleep. He flipped open his Bible to Romans 12, a passage he had read many times:

Therefore, I urge you, brothers and sisters, in view of God's mercy, to offer your bodies as a living sacrifice, holy and pleasing to God, this is your true and proper worship (Romans 12:1).

He had always thought of worship as something that happened in church with music. But this verse talked about making every day a chance to live for God.

Michael realized that being a Christian meant not just being good but giving of himself. Just like Paul said: *I am already being poured out like a drink offering* (2 Timothy 4:6).

After a few weeks, Michael saw how much of his life centered around comfort. He didn't feel guilty. He felt inspired.

He started getting up early to pray, Not because he had to, but because he wanted more of God. He offered to help a young man from church facing addiction. He and his wife decided to spend less on entertainment to support a missionary they had never met. Most importantly, he began praying a risky prayer every day. "Lord, what does obedience look like today? Whatever it is, yes."

Months later, Michael wasn't just going to church. He was living out his faith. It became his guiding force in his job, parenting, relationships, and even during tough times. He hadn't changed his whole life or moved away. But he had surrendered, and that made all the difference.

He learned that living sacrificially wasn't just a big act. It was about choosing to give a little more each day. It meant letting Christ take the lead as he stepped back (John 3:30). It involved putting aside his own desires to lift up what really mattered.

Holy Glazed Gospel Donuts

Ingredients:

- 4 cups Dough of diluted doctrine
- 2 cups Glaze of grace without truth
- 1 pinch of prosperity powder
- 3 tbsp of self-care theology

Instructions:

Fry quickly in consumer culture. Glaze heavily so nothing sticks, especially conviction.

Tip: Sweet enough to forget the cross.

Chapter 9: The Danger of Partial Truths

Key Verse: You shall know the truth, and the truth shall set you free.

(John 8:32)

Preaching only selective parts of the gospel threatens the integrity of the Christian message. By overlooking the complete story of God, we become vulnerable to accepting a weaker *sugar-coated* version of the truth that is no longer powerful or impactful. Because our human nature naturally seeks out solace and security, it's easy to understand why we gravitate to these reassuring messages. Only we set ourselves up for failure when we adopt only parts of the truth while neglecting its entirety. In our desire for peace and comfort, we often cut out sections of the gospel that may seem too difficult, uncomfortable, or controversial. This has led to the rise of what we could call *partial truths*.

Partial truths convey only part of the truth, which leads to an overall deceptive interpretation of the message. The message can be accurate in some respects but will also be misleading by omitting essential elements or by emphasizing certain parts of Scripture while ignoring others. Without the complete picture, this limited information leads to a misguided interpretations of God's message and makes one believe they have received the full gospel, when in reality, they have only endorsed a diluted version.

For example, Psalms 14:1-B says: *There is no God.* If this is true, what's the point of the Bible? However, the entire verse reads: *The fool says in his heart, There is no God.* As you can see, the complete verse tells a different story. The Bible repeatedly warns against deception. In 2 Corinthians 11:13-15, Paul describes false apostles as *masquerading as servants of righteousness.* Satan uses partial truths to distort the gospel, making it appear genuine while leading people astray. This shallow, incomplete faith often collapses under the weight of life's trials, leaving believers disillusioned and vulnerable.

Often the gospel gets reduced to a message of going-to-heaven by believing in Jesus for personal salvation, without addressing the larger implications of following Christ. The cost of discipleship or the necessity of living a transformed life are part of the process. While salvation is indeed a crucial part of the gospel message, it is not the whole story. The full gospel encompasses not only salvation but also sanctification, kingdom living, and the ultimate restoration of creation. By emphasizing salvation alone, we misrepresent God's complete plan and the demands of discipleship.

The apostle Paul recognized this danger and often warned the Church about false teachings and incomplete gospel messages. In Acts 20:27, Paul said: *For I have not hesitated to proclaim to you the whole will of God.* He understood that the gospel is not a pick-and-choose message. It must be proclaimed in its fullness to lead people into true freedom and transformation.

Prosperity gospel is one common distortion that emphasizes material wealth, health, and success as signs of God's favor. While Scripture does promise blessings and provision, this type of gospel distorts these truths by making material benefits the central focus of the Christian life. It portrays God as a cosmic vending machine of blessings based on your faith or giving. The reality of suffering, trials, and the cost of discipleship are ignored by these teachings.

In contrast, Jesus taught that following Him involves self-denial and perseverance through hardships. He said in John 16:33: *In this world you will have trouble. But take heart! I have overcome the world.* The prosperity gospel's selective focus on blessings creates unrealistic expectations, leaving believers disillusioned when they face trials. True wealth and success are found in Christ alone, not in material possessions.

Another partial truth prevalent today is the overemphasis on individualism. This view frames salvation as solely a private decision, neglecting the communal and missional aspects of the gospel. Jesus established a community of believers united by their faith and commissioned them as the Church to live as salt and light in the world. In Matthew 28:19-20,

Jesus commands His followers to make disciples of all nations, emphasizing the importance of collective growth and mission. These partial truths can lead to a narrow, self-centered faith that prioritizes personal gain over obedience to God and service to others. Fractional messages fail to capture the full scope of the gospel's transformative power, which extends beyond individuals to the renewal of all creation.

Partial truths can also create a false sense of security. When only parts of the gospel are shared, people may believe they are saved or living according to God's will yet lack a true understanding of the faith. Jesus warned in Matthew 7:21-23 that not everyone who calls Him *Lord* will enter the kingdom of heaven, but only those who do the will of the Father. Outward religiosity or verbal affirmations of faith are not enough. True salvation requires a relationship with Christ and obedience to His full teachings.

For example, emphasizing God's love and forgiveness without addressing repentance and holiness can lead people to believe they can live however they please without consequences. Similarly, focusing on blessings while ignoring the reality of suffering can leave believers unprepared when trials come.

Partial truths lacking depth and resilience contribute to the development of a shallow faith that often prioritizes emotional satisfaction, personal gain, or social acceptance over obedience to God. Jesus illustrated this in the parable of the sower in Matthew 13:3-9. The seed that falls on rocky ground represents those who receive the Word with joy but fall away when trouble arises because they lack deep roots. A partial gospel creates this kind of fragile faith that leaves individuals spiritually stagnant, vulnerable to doubt, and disconnected from the transformative power of the gospel. Without a complete understanding of God's Word, believers are unprepared for the hardships when their faith is tested.

For the Church to thrive and fulfill its mission, it must commit to proclaiming the whole counsel of God. Teaching both the comforting and convicting aspects of Scripture emphasizes grace alongside repentance, presenting God's love in harmony with His holiness. The gospel is not merely a feel-good message. It is a call to transformation, sacrifice, and a life of obedience.

Paul's words to the Ephesian elders in Acts 20:26-27 highlight the importance of preaching the full gospel: *I declare to you today that I am innocent of the blood of any of you. For I have not hesitated to proclaim to you the whole will of God.* To withhold parts of the gospel is to leave people in spiritual danger. (Not telling people how to go to Heaven is actually telling them to go to hell).

When people reject sound doctrine in favor of partial truths, they open themselves up to deception and spiritual ruin. The Church must resist the temptation to dilute the message of Christ to make it more appealing or less controversial. This leads to a distorted view of God, misplaced faith, and ultimately, eternal separation from Him. As stated earlier, Paul warns in 2 Timothy 4:3-4: *For the time will come when people will not put up with sound doctrine. Instead, to suit their own desires, they will gather around them a great number of teachers to say what their itching ears want to hear.*

The gospel is a message of grace, but it is also a call to repentance, holiness, and transformation. Only by embracing the full Gospel can we experience the true freedom and abundant life that Christ offers. The sobering reality is that partial truths can leave people believing they are following Christ when they are not. As believers, we must commit to living out and proclaiming the whole gospel, even when it clashes with our desires or makes us uncomfortable, so that others may know the truth that truly sets them free.

Truth is not subjective or shaped by personal preferences, biases, or cultural trends, but rather objective, eternal, and unchanging. Jesus declared in John 14:6: *I am the way, the truth, and the life. No one comes to the Father except through me.* Jesus embodies ultimate truth as God's revelation in human form.

The complete gospel encompasses more than facts about Jesus' life, death, and resurrection. It also shapes our understanding of the world, the human condition, and God's plan of salvation. This life-changing knowledge frees us from sin and the lies of the enemy. Jesus affirmed this in John 8:32: *You shall know the truth, and the truth shall set you free.*

Questions

1. Do I seek God's whole truth from the Word, or do I only gravitate toward the teachings that focus on the parts I like?

2. What can I do to help others understand the full gospel?

3. How can I create opportunities for Bible study and develop conversations about what it really means to follow Christ?

4. How can I encourage my church community to hunger for solid biblical teaching?

Robert

Robert straightened his collar and walked into a popular church downtown for the first time. A friend had invited him and couldn't stop talking about the lively worship, the messages, and how uplifting it all felt.

Curiosity got to him. He had grown up in a traditional church where sermons felt long, awkward, and often heavy. Recently though, he had drifted away from his faith. Life felt messy and his job was exhausting, his relationships felt shallow, and spiritually he felt drained.

"Maybe this is what I need," he thought.

The music was powerful, with big screens showing bright lyrics and visuals. The crowd was engaged, hands up, hearts open.

The pastor walked up, confident and relatable, wearing a big smile. "God has something big for you!" he said. "Your setback is a setup for your comeback! You were born to rise above!"

The sermon was upbeat, funny, packed with uplifting stories. Scripture was mentioned here and there but mostly served as a backdrop to the motivation.

The main message was clear: God wants you happy and successful. Don't let anyone tell you different.

People clapped, laughed, and cried.

But Robert stayed quiet.

Inside, he felt empty.

On the way home, Robert thought back on the sermon. It felt good and positive, but something was off.

The pastor never talked about sin. There was no mention of the cross or repentance.

Robert remembered Jesus' words from Luke 9:23: *If anyone wants to follow me, let him deny himself and take up his cross daily.*

But that wasn't touched on in the sermon. It was all about discovering yourself, not denying yourself. No real talk about the cost of following Jesus, just the benefits. It wasn't that the message was wrong, it was just incomplete.

He recalled Paul's warning to Timothy: *For the time will come when they will not endure sound teaching, but will gather teachers to suit their own desires* (2 Timothy 4:3).

He thought about how sugar gives a quick boost but can leave you feeling worse later. That's what the sermon did. It stirred him up but didn't fill his soul.

The issue with these sweet sermons, wasn't that they were always lying, it's that they shared only part of the truth, robbing the listener of what they really need.

He realized:

You can preach hope without holiness.

Preach grace without repentance.

Preach purpose without surrender.

Preach Jesus as a life coach but not as Lord.

And people will eat it up. They'll keep coming back, but they won't change. Not really.

That night, Robert opened his Bible. Not out of guilt. But out of hunger.

He started reading through the Gospels again. This time he noticed not just the miracles but the calls to repent, the confrontations with sin, the urgency of faith, and warnings about being lukewarm.

Jesus didn't offer a simple message. He told the rich young man to sell everything. He scolded Peter for resisting the cross. He warned that the path is narrow and few find it. He told his followers to count the cost, to sacrifice their lives to save them.

Yet he also promised them a full life but only after surrender.

Robert began to cry. He realized what he truly needed wasn't a sugary boost but a full meal.

In the following weeks, Robert made some changes. He stopped chasing popular churches and started looking for ones that taught the whole truth. He started asking tough questions about the messages he heard:

Did they lead to repentance?

Did they point to the cross?

Did they lift up Christ or just me?

He surrounded himself with knowledgeable believers who were not afraid to share honest hard truths.

Slowly, he started to grow spiritually. The Word began to reshape his mind. Conviction softened his heart.

God's truth, sharp and real, changed the way he thought, lived, and loved. He wasn't just going to church anymore. He was becoming a disciple.

Robert learned that the full gospel isn't always comfy, but it's always good. It does more than inspire, it changes lives. It doesn't just add decoration to your life, it rebuilds you from the inside. It doesn't shy away from hard truths, it lays them out with love, offering real grace and a Savior who saves us.

Cupcake Conversion Crumble

Ingredients:

- 3 cups Cake mix of easy-believism
- No eggs of endurance needed
- 1 tbsp sugar substitute for discipleship
- Heavily frost with "you're enough" slogans

Instructions:

Bake at low commitment. Crumbles under the weight of real trials.

Warning: Not built to last.

CHAPTER 10

Chapter 10: Breaking Free from Sugar-coated Sermons

Key Verse: Now I commit you to God and to the word of

his grace, which can build you up and give you an

inheritance among all those who are sanctified.

(Acts 20:32)

The early Church prioritized preaching the full counsel of God, addressing both the blessings of salvation and the cost of following Jesus. Today, many churches avoid difficult topics to appeal to preferences and avoid offense. This diluted teaching leaves believers in spiritual immaturity, unprepared for life's challenges and the demands of discipleship. Without a solid foundation in Scripture, believers are vulnerable to deception, confusion, and a false sense of security. Paul warns in Ephesians 4:14 that immature believers are *tossed back and forth by the waves* of false teaching.

In Matthew 7:21-23, Jesus warns that many will claim to follow Him will be rejected because they did not live according to His will.

Pursuing solid, biblical teaching requires embracing all of God's Word, even when it challenges your desires. This is the only path to true transformation and spiritual growth.

To grow in faith and avoid the dangers of sugar-coated sermons, you must intentionally pursue sound doctrine and biblical truth. Here are four practical steps:

1. Read and Study the Bible Regularly

Scripture is the ultimate source of truth and reveals God's full counsel. By reading and meditating on God's Word, we begin to understand His heart, His plan of salvation, and the way in which He calls us to live. A strong foundation in Scripture strengthens your faith and helps you embrace the gospel fully, even when it challenges you. It also provides us with the nourishment we need to avoid the emptiness of sugar-coated sermons. When we develop a consistent habit of reading and studying the Bible and immersing ourselves in Scripture, we will become more attuned to the voice of God and more willing to embrace the full gospel, even when it challenges us.

If you've never read the Bible before, a good place to start is the book of John.

2. Seek Sound Preaching

Sound preaching addresses the entirety of the Bible, including both its blessings and its demands. Find a church that prioritizes Scripture over entertainment or feel-good messages. Ask yourself: Does this sermon challenge me to grow in my faith? Does it address the deeper issues of sin, repentance, and sanctification? Does it align with Scripture, or does it avoid difficult truths? Faithful preaching promotes spiritual growth, even when it is uncomfortable.

3. Engage in Community and Accountability

Church should be a place where we come together to worship God, grow in our understanding of His Word, and hold one another accountable. Find and join a grounded community of believers who are committed to seeking the truth and willing to speak that truth to one another as well as committed to living out the full gospel and supporting each other through difficult times. When we are part of a healthy, biblically grounded community, we are less likely to be swept away by shallow teachings and more likely to remain rooted in the truth of God's Word.

4. Embrace the Full Gospel

The true gospel is both comforting and confronting. It declares God's immeasurable love and grace while calling us to repentance, obedience, and self-denial. It assures us of forgiveness, but it also demands a new way of living. Salvation is a free gift through Jesus Christ, but it comes at a cost. Jesus gave His life for you, and He calls you to surrender your life to Him in return. So embrace the entire gospel, not just the parts that are easy to hear or emotionally uplifting.

The fullness of the gospel begins with the recognition that we are sinners in need of a Savior. This solid doctrine transforms your heart and mind. It leads to character growth, conviction, and renewed purpose. When you stop seeking messages that cater to your preferences and start seeking the truths of Scripture, your faith deepens. Following Christ means allowing His Word to reshape your life rather than trying to fit Christianity into your lifestyle.

Sugar-coated sermons fail to produce mature, faithful disciples. To grow in faith you must pursue sound doctrine, study Scripture, and embrace the gospel in its fullness. True transformation comes when you allow God's Word to challenge, convict, and change you.

Questions

1. Do you have a time set aside to read and study your Bible daily?

2. Are you listening to genuinely Biblical sermons and lessons?

3. Are you associated with a group of believers who hold you accountable when you mess up?

4. Are you embracing the whole gospel?

James

James was a thirty-two year-old graphic designer living in a fast-paced city. Burnt out from work and disillusioned with life, he felt an emptiness gnawing at his soul. One Sunday morning, on a whim, he decided to attend a church that several of his coworkers had raved about. "You'll love it," one had said. "It's positive, uplifting, and never judgmental."

As James walked into the sleek, modern sanctuary, he was greeted with warm smiles and the aroma of artisan coffee. The music was energetic, the lights were dazzling, and everything seemed perfectly choreographed. The preacher stepped onstage, charismatic and relatable, dressed in jeans and sneakers.

His sermon was titled *You Were Made for More*. He spoke about dreams, purpose, and unlocking potential. He told stories of people overcoming obstacles and living their best lives. He quoted a few Bible verses mostly from Proverbs and Psalms but James noticed something odd. There was no mention of sin. No talk of repentance. No cross. No Christ crucified. Everything was polished and pleasant. But strangely, James left the service feeling hollow. "Is this all there is to Christianity?" he wondered. "Where was the depth? The challenge? The truth?"

Over the next few weeks James kept attending. The messages were always cheerful, always affirming. They sounded good but never good enough to satisfy the ache in his soul. One night, feeling deeply convicted, he picked up a Bible he hadn't touched in years. As he read the Gospels, he was struck by Jesus' words:

Whoever wants to be my disciple must deny themselves and take up their cross and follow me (Matthew 16:24).

Unless you repent, you too will all perish (Luke 13:3).

If the world hates you, keep in mind that it hated me first (John 15:18).

Tears filled his eyes. This was the Jesus he had heard about on Sunday mornings. Not the life coach, not the motivational speaker but the Savior who called people to die to themselves and be born again. James realized he had been fed spiritual candy. What he needed was the Bread of Life.

Truth-Free Trifle

Ingredients:

- Layers of light anecdotes
- Cool Whip of charisma
- Jam of juicy promises
- No Scripture foundation
- A dash of spiritual ambiguity

Instructions:

Build in a glass dish of personality. Spoon-feed slowly, skipping hard teachings.

Serving Suggestion: Best served to crowds, not disciples.

CHAPTER 11

Chapter 11: From Sugar Cookies to Bread of Life

Key Verse: Jesus answered, 'I am the bread of life. Whoever comes to me will never go hungry, and whoever believes in me will never be thirsty.'

(John 6:35)

Jesus is The Bread of Life. He stands in sharp contrast to sugar-coated teachings. Unlike feel-good messages that fail to nourish or transform, His words offer real sustenance and eternal hope. A sugary gospel may provide fleeting comfort, but it leaves people spiritually empty. Returning to Jesus means embracing the deep truths only He can provide, truths that meet the soul's deepest needs.

The Church today faces a crisis of spiritual malnourishment. Many seek the fast food of instant gratification and surface-level comfort. Sugar-coated sermons cater to this desire, offering temporary satisfaction without feeding the deeper issues of the heart. These shallow teachings leave believers spiritually hungry, longing for something more substantial.

People are not simply hungry for comfort or emotional highs. They are hungry for truth.

In John 6:35, Jesus says: *I am the bread of life. Whoever comes to me will never go hungry, and whoever believes in me will never be thirsty.*

When Jesus calls Himself the *Bread of Life* He identifies as the only true source of spiritual nourishment. Just as bread sustains the body, Jesus sustains the soul. This was not a promise of physical provision but an invitation to receive the spiritual sustenance only He can provide. Jesus offers Himself as the eternal source of life, capable of satisfying the deepest hunger and thirst of the human heart.

This statement is not just a metaphor. It's a deep, theological declaration that speaks to the very essence of who Jesus is and what He offers to those who follow Him. To understand this claim, it is important to consider its context. Earlier in John 6, Jesus miraculously fed five thousand people with five loaves and two fish. While this act met their physical needs, it pointed to a greater spiritual truth. The crowd, amazed by the miracle, sought more signs, but Jesus redirected their focus. He invited them to seek the true bread that feeds the soul and grants eternal life.

Through His life, death, and resurrection, Jesus provides the fulfillment that nothing else can. Unlike the fleeting sweetness of sugar-coated sermons, His nourishment is eternal. Jesus offers abiding peace, joy, and strength that transcend circumstances. He provides a relationship with God rooted in grace, truth, and love, enabling believers to endure trials with faithfulness.

Jesus highlights two key actions required to receive this nourishment: coming to Him and believing in Him.

To *come* to Jesus is to approach Him in faith and enter into a personal relationship with Him. It requires acknowledging your need for His grace and provision, rather than admiring Him from a distance.

To *believe* in Him means placing your trust and reliance on Him as the Savior who died for your sins and rose again to give you new life. Belief is more than intellectual agreement. It's a deep trust in Jesus as the only one who can satisfy your spiritual hunger and thirst.

Look at these steps as if you were physically starving (sin). You're losing muscle. Your cheeks are sunken. Your body is dying. Your hunger pangs are so strong all you can think about is food (you realize your lost state of existence). You seek out anything to eat. Only bugs and grass don't provide enough nutrition (sugar-coated sermons). You see a farmer with a food stand selling produce, only you have no money. You're at the farmer's mercy. You approach the farmer, acknowledge your dire condition, and ask for compassion. You say you'll even take the goods others rejected (acknowledging your sinful condition). Only the farmer asks to take you to his house to eat. You have to believe he will do what he says and not harm you in order to go with him (belief). He takes you home and serves you a twelve course meal (God's mercy and grace of salvation). You are so grateful to the farmer that you eagerly go to work in his fields and tend his flocks (discipleship).

This invitation is open to everyone. Regardless of background, status, or past, Jesus offers Himself as the Bread of Life to all who come and believe. He promises to fill the deepest longings of your soul and provide eternal nourishment that cannot be found anywhere else.

Jesus' words remind us that only He can meet the spiritual needs of a world searching for truth and fulfillment. While sugar-coated teachings may attract attention, they cannot sustain or transform. True nourishment comes from the Bread of Life, who offers lasting hope, peace, and purpose.

Questions

1. Are you feasting on the empty calories of a sugar-coated gospel, or are you feasting on the nutrient rich Word of God?

2. Are there parts of your life that reflect spiritual malnourishment?

3. What is one practical step you can take this week to move away from spiritual "fast food" and toward the eternal sustenance Jesus offers?

4. When I feel spiritually empty, do I run first to Jesus or to temporary comforts?

5. Am I truly satisfied in Christ, or am I still chasing after other sources of fulfillment?

Cameron

Cameron always thought of himself as a spiritual guy. Growing up in church, he could recite the Bible verses and fit in at any Christian gathering. After college, he wandered a bit trying out self-help books, listening to prosperity podcasts, and following trendy ministries on Instagram that mixed feel-good ideas with flashy visuals.

Every Sunday he watched the livestream from a big megachurch. The messages were slick and packed with catchy lines like: God's got big plans for you! Speak your breakthrough into existence! You are enough!

He liked the upbeat vibes. It felt like a nice boost for the week. But by Monday morning that energy faded.

Even with all the positive messages, Cameron felt oddly empty. The excitement just didn't last. The anxiety, guilt, and that nagging feeling in his heart always came back.

One night, while browsing YouTube, he found an old video of a preacher talking about John 6. This wasn't a flashy preacher, just a guy with a Bible, speaking with genuine conviction.

"Jesus said to them, 'I am the bread of life. Whoever comes to me shall not hunger, and whoever believes in me shall never thirst." (John 6:35).

Cameron stopped and thought. Bread of life? What did that even mean?

The preacher explained how Jesus had just fed a big crowd with bread and fish. The people were amazed and came back wanting more food the next day. But Jesus wasn't just about filling them up. He challenged them," You are looking for me not because you saw the signs, but because you ate your fill of the loaves" (John 6:26).

The preacher's tone intensified. "Jesus didn't just come to give out more bread, He came to be their Bread. He wasn't there for comfort food; He offered Himself for their souls."

Cameron was taken aback. He realized he had been chasing comfort instead of Christ. He wanted a boost, not a change. He'd filled his life with easy spiritual feel-good snack sermons, soft promises, and nice ideas that never really addressed sin or called for change.

That night Cameron started to rethink the messages he had been consuming. They were smooth to digest, but they didn't last. They pushed success instead of surrender, pleasure instead of purity, and a Jesus who solved problems without asking for commitment.

John 6 was too tough, too direct. Jesus talked about what it really means to follow Him saying, "Unless you eat of my flesh and drink of my blood..." Cameron realized he had been avoiding the true Jesus. He wasn't always easy. But He was real. And that was what his soul craved.

Cameron started going to a smaller church that really preached all of the Bible. It wasn't fancy, and the pastor wasn't a social media star, but the sermons were packed with Scripture. Jesus was front and center, and the full gospel was shared: sin, repentance, grace, giving up self, and a new life in Christ.

Though it wasn't always about feeling good, it started to fill him up.

He found himself crying at the altar from a deep sense of holiness.

The Word didn't just inspire him. It moved him in a way that cut and healed at the same time.

Jesus became more than just a Sunday message or a quick fix. He became Cameron's daily nourishment. His true fulfillment. His Bread of Life

Cameron's prayer each morning is: Lord, feed me with truth. Break me if you must. Just don't let me starve on lies.

The Bread of Life Loaf

Ingredients:

- 1 Savior (Jesus Christ)
- 3 cups Faith
- 2 cups Obedience
- 1 tbsp Daily Cross
- ½ cup Trust in Trials
- Whole grain Word of God

Instructions :

Mix all in the vessel of surrender.
Let rise with prayer.
Bake with the fire of God's presence.
Break and share with others.

Best served: Daily at the table of communion.

Conclusion

As we reach the end of this book, it is clear that the modern Church really needs a change. Not in the structure of the gospel but in its heart. It needs to be willing to surrender. What we really need isn't a flashy new plan but a comeback to the solid ground of genuine faith. Maybe the Church doesn't need a new recipe, maybe it needs less sugar and more salt.

This sugar-coated Christianity skips the tough truths, making it easier to swallow. This version offers comfort without real conviction, blessings without obedience, and inspiration without transformation. It might fill up seats and stimulate emotions, but it doesn't bring the lasting power that truly saves and transforms.

We looked at how this softening has changed the modern Church today. We have seen the shift from focusing on truth to being flexible, from seeking depth to just entertainment, and from committed discipleship to quiet consumers. A lot of churches have sadly traded the true gospel for a message that's more appealing to flesh and not the soul.

These decorated shallow sermons might inspire but not convict. They comfort but don't correct. The Church needs to revisit the full message of God. Not only the parts about grace but also the hard truths about judgment, repentance, holiness, and sacrifice. The true gospel is not just a set of beliefs. It's a call to put aside our own desires, follow Jesus, and take up our crosses every day, becoming more like Him.

The core of the message is the cross. It shows us that what Christ did for us is enough and that being a Christian means to surrender all. Sadly, some churches have swapped deep teachings for flashy emotional entertainment, creating congregations that are stirred but not shaken in their faith.

We need to feed the Church the full meal of Scripture instead of a sweet spiritual snack. True repentance is the first ingredient for transformation. Without it faith has a bitter taste. God's Word calls each of us to put aside our own will so that Christ can satisfy our hunger.

The Great Commission is not about gathering big crowds but about making real disciples who truly know, love, and obey Jesus. Following Christ isn't meant to be easy. It's supposed to be a holy challenge, putting aside our own pleasures and pride.

Knowing part of the truth is not enough. A sugar-coated gospel is not good news at all. It leads to deception, stagnation, and ultimately, to separation from Christ. Being faithful to the true gospel means sharing the whole truth, the good, the bad and the ugly. The truth is what sets us free.

Jesus, the true Bread of Life, is our only real source of fulfillment. Emotion filled entertainment might satisfy for a moment, but only Christ can keep us fed for eternity.

Every chapter has been a wake-up call to step away from cultural compromises and turn back to Jesus wholeheartedly as our Lord and Savior. The Church cannot afford to keep sugar-coating the gospel hoping to draw a crowd. We need to share a gospel that draws people to the Cross, even if that means losing followers, offending the world and emptying buildings.

The early Church did not change the world by entertaining people. They changed the world by standing firm with the

Word of God by putting Christ first. They didn't rely on sweet, feel-good speeches. They simply offered Christ crucified.

This is not the ending. It is a moment of choice.

- Are you willing to stick to the full truth of God's Word, even when it's tough?

- Will you boldly teach the hard truths, even if they offend?

- Are you ready to create disciples who will put aside their own lives to fully follow Christ?

- Will you let go of cultural conformity for the greater good of the kingdom?

Key terms used in this book.

Making Sugar Cookies

The process of making a gospel message that is too sweet, appealing, and easy to digest but lacks spiritual wisdom and nourishment. Like sugar cookies, these messages are simple and designed to satisfy surface-level cravings without addressing deeper spiritual needs or fostering lasting transformation.

Also known as: Oversimplified teachings, Feel-good doctrines, Pleasure tailored messages, Quick fixes for deeper spiritual hunger.

Sugar-Coated Gospel

A version of the Christian gospel that emphasizes only the comforting, positive parts, such as love, blessings, and grace, while avoiding or downplaying difficult truths like sin, repentance, judgment, and the cost of discipleship. It lacks the full depth of the biblical message and often leads to shallow faith.

Watered-Down Gospel

A diluted version of the gospel that minimizes or omits critical truths such as sin, repentance, judgment, and the cost of discipleship. It prioritizes comfort, acceptance, and ease over the full message of Scripture, leaving listeners with a shallow understanding of faith. Like water added to juice, it reduces the potency and richness of the original message.

Alternatives are: Diluted doctrine, Softened truth, Incomplete gospel, Compromised teaching, Half-truth messages, Weak theology, Shallow spirituality, Gospel without substance.

No Added Conviction

Refers to a message that avoids the challenging work of conviction. Conviction, prompted by the Holy Spirit, is the deep and often uncomfortable awareness of one's sin or need for change. A gospel without conviction fails to call people to repentance or transformation, offering comfort without responsibility.

Sprinkles on Top
A metaphor for superficial elements added to a watered-down gospel message. Sprinkles are sweet and decorative but lack any real substance or nourishment. This term describes the use of catchy phrases, entertaining stories, or motivational slogans to make a message more appealing, while neglecting deeper spiritual truths.

These include: Empty embellishments, Superficial add-ons, Surface-level sweetness, Feel-good fluff, Gospel glitter

Candy Coating
A glossy, sweet presentation of the gospel that hides the harder truths beneath a layer of comforting words. It attracts attention but lacks the substance needed for true spiritual growth.

Frosting Without the Cake
A message that focuses on external appeal without providing the foundational truths of the gospel. Like frosting without cake, it may look appealing but lacks the core substance.

Cotton Candy Theology
A gospel presentation that feels good in the moment but fades quickly, leaving no lasting impact. It offers sweetness without substance, addressing surface-level desires while ignoring deeper spiritual needs.

Decorated Emptiness
A message that is outwardly attractive but lacks depth or transformative power. It may be filled with uplifting sentiments but fails to address sin, repentance, or the call to discipleship.

Hollow Hype
Describes exaggerated or excessive enthusiastic presentations of the gospel that focus on excitement and emotional appeal rather than truth. It leaves people spiritually unfulfilled and unprepared for real challenges.

Cosmetic Preaching
Preaching that prioritizes presentation over content. It focuses on audio/video production rather than delivering truth. The result is a surface-level faith that lacks depth and conviction.

Confetti Truth
A scattered, fragmented approach to the gospel that highlights only the fun or joyous parts while ignoring the weightier matters of sin, judgment, and obedience. It entertains but does not convert.

Remember

The central warning of *Making Sugar Cookies* is clear: It may taste sweet in the moment, but its bitterness will last forever.

In life, we approach faith like dessert. We sample only what seems delightful. Just as a diet of pure sugar weakens the body over time, a steady diet of feel-good sermons without biblical truth leaves the soul spiritually weak. In a true gospel recipe every ingredient matters. Leave out repentance, obedience, or discipleship, and the result may look appealing but lacks the substance to maintain a faithful Christian life.

Repentance Revival Pie

Ingredients:

- 2 cups brokenness over sin (Psalm 51:17)
- 1 ½ cups genuine confession (1 John 1:9)
- ¾ cup turning away (Acts 3:19)
- Dash of godly sorrow (2 Corinthians 7:10)
- Crust made from grace and mercy (Ephesians 2:8-9)

Instructions:

Mix brokenness and confession until the dough of the heart
Softens.
Stir in turning away from sin.
Pour into the crust of grace.
Bake under the refining heat of the Holy Spirit.
Best served fresh at the altar of surrender.

Disciple's Daily Delight

Ingredients:

- 2 cups of the Word (2 Timothy 3:16-17)
- 1 heaping scoop of obedience (John 14:15)
- ½ cup prayerful meditation (Psalm 1:2)
- 1 tbsp of bold witness (Acts 1:8)
- 1 handshake of fellowship (Hebrews 10:25)

Instructions:

Combine the Word and obedience for a strong base.
Blend in daily meditation and prayer.
Fold in witness and fellowship.
Let simmer in the joy of the Lord.
Consume daily for strength, direction, and spiritual nourishment.

Cross-Bearing Brownies

Ingredients:

- 1 cup surrender (Galatians 2:20)
- ½ cup hardship (2 Timothy 3:12)
- ¾ cup perseverance (James 1:2-4)
- 1 teaspoon joy in suffering (Romans 5:3-5)
- A dash of eternal hope (Colossians 1:27)

Instructions:

Mix all ingredients, even the bitter ones.
Bake under pressure for a deeper, richer result.
Cool with perspective of eternity.
Serve with grace, and share with those walking difficult roads.

Additional Personal Experiences

Frank

Frank grew up in a small town where going to church on Sundays was just what families did. When he moved to the city for a job, he looked for a church that reminded him of home. He quickly found one. It had a cool, modern building, friendly people at the door, and music that made you want to move. The sermons were always interesting and packed with stories, jokes, and sayings that made you feel good. Every week, he left feeling happy and sure that God wanted him to have a good life.

But after a while, Frank started feeling like something was missing. When he struggled with things he kept secret or couldn't make up his mind about something important, the sermons didn't really help. They said, "God loves you just the way you are!" He couldn't even remember the last time he heard the word "sorry" or felt like he needed to check himself. At a men's group, when Frank talked about what he was going through, the others just nodded and said, "Don't worry, God wants you to be happy!"

One Sunday, Frank went with a friend to an older church. The service was simpler, the songs were quieter, and the sermon was from the book of Mark. The pastor talked openly about how Jesus wants us to "say no to ourselves, carry our cross, and follow Him." He chatted about what it means to really follow Jesus and how good it feels to give everything to Him. The message made Frank uncomfortable. He felt bad about things he'd been ignoring for years.

After the service, Frank asked the pastor why he didn't preach more happy messages. The pastor smiled kindly. "The real message isn't always easy to hear, but it's the only way to really live and change for good. Messages that just make you feel good can't fix a person. Jesus can but He wants us to be sorry, believe, and follow Him."

That talk stayed with Frank. He realized that the easy kind of Christianity had kept him from growing spiritually. He never asked himself tough questions or really tried to get better. He started reading the Bible on his own, wanting to find truth that would both challenge and encourage him. Slowly, Frank's faith grew stronger. He learned that God's love was bigger than he thought, but it also meant he needed to change.

Frank found a new church that preached everything God had to say, even when it was hard. He learned how good it feels to really be sorry and how strong grace is. As he grew, Frank started telling others to look for the real story, not just messages that made them feel good. He knew now that only the truth could make them free.

Mia

Mia entered the church, carrying a familiar burden. She hadn't attended in a few weeks. Missing her usual routine left her with a sense of emptiness. The pews were nearly full as she settled into a seat at the back. It was a typical Sunday morning, filled with warmth and friendliness.

Pastor Chris stood at the front, smiling broadly, as if ready to share an important message. "Good morning, everyone!" he said loudly, with cheer in his voice. "I hope you're ready to receive God's love today."

Mia felt uneasy in her seat. She usually found comfort in Pastor Chris' words but today felt different. God's love was why she came to church, but she needed more. She was dealing with life's struggles, questioning her purpose, and facing a career setback, leaving her feeling empty. She longed for words that addressed real, everyday problems.

Pastor Chris continued, "God's love is unconditional. It's not about your achievements or mistakes. You are enough as you are. Accept it, and your life will change." His words felt soothing, like a bandage on an unhealed wound but the comfort didn't last.

While God's love is indeed unconditional, his words didn't touch on life's hard parts like doubts and difficult questions. Love sometimes requires growth, not just comfort. "As you leave today," Pastor Chris said, "remember, you can achieve your dreams because God wants the best for you. Claim your blessing today!"

Mia felt the weight of this promise, sensing it was too optimistic, like receiving a lottery ticket with expectations of an easy win, while ignoring the effort needed to change one's circumstances. Others in the congregation seemed uplifted, nodding with hope. They wanted to believe that just having faith would make everything alright.

Mia wasn't convinced it was enough for her. Her thoughts drifted. Life isn't just about accepting God's love and waiting for everything to be okay. It involves confronting the hard parts, the failures, struggles, and the unexpected. It's about perseverance and finding meaning in tough times, balancing trust in God with taking action to change what can be changed.

As Pastor Chris ended his sermon, the music began a slow, cheerful tune and everyone stood up, clapping and moving with the rhythm. Mia stayed seated briefly, reflecting with her hands resting in her lap. She sensed the room's optimism but felt untouched by it. She desired more from the sermon, maybe something realistic, not just comforting.

When the service concluded, people left, discussing how the sermon inspired them. Mia lingered, observing them, pondering if they felt faith went beyond easy promises of success and happiness. Quietly, she left the church, still struggling with the emptiness that the sermon hadn't filled.

Pastor Chris encouraged many, but Mia sought something more challenging. She wanted to face what she had been avoiding in her life. True transformation doesn't happen by just feeling good. It requires facing difficult truths. Mia realized she would keep searching. Not for simple answers, but for something real. Something to help her progress, even when the path was uncertain.

Tom

Tom had always been wary of churches. Raised in a small town with a fire-and-brimstone preacher, his childhood church had always felt like a place of guilt rather than grace. When he got older, he had stopped attending altogether, choosing to explore spirituality in quieter, less judgmental ways. But when his friend Sarah invited him to a church she'd recently joined, he agreed, thinking it would at least be a chance to catch up with her.

The moment Tom stepped inside, he felt like he had entered a different world. The building was modern, gleaming white with oversized windows that let in the light, and the air smelled like fresh coffee and new carpet. There were no dark wooden pews. The room had soft blue lights throughout, The low sound of chatter filled the air, as though people were gathering for a social event rather than a sacred service.

What struck Tom the most was the music. The church had a full band, with drums, electric guitars, and a female vocalist who seemed to float above the congregation. When the service began, the band struck up the first chords of a song, and Tom felt an unexpected wave of emotion rise up in his chest. The music was so smooth, so polished. It was the kind of music you would hear on the radio. It was uplifting, catchy, and effortlessly engaging. People stood, swayed, and lifted their hands as the words of the song swirled around him.

The lyrics were sweet and simple, echoing the familiar themes of love, hope, and God's grace. *I am chosen, I am free, I am living for eternity.* The singer's voice soared effortlessly, and the congregation responded with joy, as if they were participating in a celebration, not worship. For a moment, it felt like he was at a concert, not a church.

Tom found himself caught between admiration and discomfort. The music was undeniably beautiful, but it felt too easy. Like a sugary coating, too perfect, too comforting. There was no rawness to it, no struggle. Where were the haunting hymns that had once made him sit in reverence, contemplating the depth of faith and hardship? Where were the songs that shook him out of complacency? This music felt almost too manufactured, too polished, as if it had been carefully designed to bypass the mind and go straight for the heart.

The people around him were caught up in it. Their eyes closed. Their hands raised. Their faces glowed with emotion.

Tom couldn't help but wonder: were they feeling something deeper, or had they just been swept away by the sheer force of the music's sweetness? Was this worship, or just a beautiful distraction?

As the service progressed, another song, just as smooth, just as cheerful. And then another, with the same repetitive, syrupy lyrics. By the time the sermon started, Tom felt oddly fatigued, as if he had been in a sugar rush, high on the sweetness of it all but unsure what it was really sustaining him through.

When the service ended, the congregation was excited with a sense of fulfillment. People greeted each other with smiles and laughter. Their eyes were bright with a kind of warmth that Tom hadn't seen in a long time. He couldn't deny there was something magnetic about it. The music had created an atmosphere that was impossible to ignore, a kind of emotional high that everyone seemed to share.

Walking out of the church, Tom turned to Sarah, who was chatting excitedly about the service. "It was... nice," he said slowly, choosing his words carefully. "The music was great, but it almost felt... too smooth. Like it was made to make us feel good but without asking anything hard of us. Does that make sense?"

Sarah nodded, her face softening. "I get what you mean. It's different from what you're used to, I think. But for me, it's comforting. It reminds me of the good things, of God's love, and that's what I need right now."

Tom didn't have an answer for that. He knew he was still carrying his own baggage, his doubts, his skepticism, but something about the experience stuck with him. He wasn't sure if it was the music or the ease with which people had given themselves to it. But there was something there. Something easy. Something that made him question whether he had been making things harder on himself than they needed to be.

For the first time in a long while, Tom found himself wondering: What if the sweetness, the easy music, was part of the answer? What if the faith he had been avoiding all this time didn't have to come with struggle? What if it was, after all, a little more like the songs with the perfect harmony of hope and peace?

But then again, maybe it was too easy. Maybe faith couldn't be sugar-coated.

www.ingramcontent.com/pod-product-compliance
Lightning Source LLC
Chambersburg PA
CBHW070842120626
46556CB00002B/846